Entangled Memories in the Global South

Series Editors
Jie-Hyun Lim
Department of History and the Critical
Global Studies Institute
Sogang University
Seoul, Korea (Republic of)

Eve Rosenhaft
School of Histories, Languages & Cultures
University of Liverpool
Liverpool, UK

This book series offers new perspectives on the past and present of global memory formation. Recognizing the impact of globalization on collective memory, the titles in the series explore how memories have become entangled, reconciled, contested, conflicted and negotiated across borders, connecting historical actors and events across time and space in new ways. In particular, the books in this series examine the de-territorialization of mnemonic discourse on colonialism, war and genocide since World War II. The focus of the series is the Global South, defined not simply by geography but by the interactions within regions and polities between majority and minority, dominant and subaltern, native and immigrant actors and bearers of distinct historical experiences. The series builds on recent developments in memory studies scholarship, drawing on and going beyond such concepts as multidirectional, travelling, cosmopolitan, entangled and prosthetic. It takes a broadly historical approach to the understanding of how national collective memories have become interconnected through such processes as cross-referencing, imitation and competition and encourages critical reflection on their consequences.

More information about this series at
http://www.palgrave.com/gp/series/16450

Jie-Hyun Lim • Eve Rosenhaft
Editors

Mnemonic Solidarity

Global Interventions

Editors
Jie-Hyun Lim
Department of History and the
Critical Global Studies Institute
Sogang University
Seoul, Korea (Republic of)

Eve Rosenhaft
School of Histories, Languages &
Cultures
University of Liverpool
Liverpool, UK

ISSN 2662-5687 ISSN 2662-5695 (electronic)
Entangled Memories in the Global South
ISBN 978-3-030-57668-4 ISBN 978-3-030-57669-1 (eBook)
https://doi.org/10.1007/978-3-030-57669-1

© The Editor(s) (if applicable) and The Author(s) 2021. This book is an open access publication.
Open Access This book is licensed under the terms of the Creative Commons Attribution 4.0 International License (http://creativecommons.org/licenses/by/4.0/), which permits use, sharing, adaptation, distribution and reproduction in any medium or format, as long as you give appropriate credit to the original author(s) and the source, provide a link to the Creative Commons licence and indicate if changes were made.
The images or other third party material in this book are included in the book's Creative Commons licence, unless indicated otherwise in a credit line to the material. If material is not included in the book's Creative Commons licence and your intended use is not permitted by statutory regulation or exceeds the permitted use, you will need to obtain permission directly from the copyright holder.
The use of general descriptive names, registered names, trademarks, service marks, etc. in this publication does not imply, even in the absence of a specific statement, that such names are exempt from the relevant protective laws and regulations and therefore free for general use.
The publisher, the authors and the editors are safe to assume that the advice and information in this book are believed to be true and accurate at the date of publication. Neither the publisher nor the authors or the editors give a warranty, expressed or implied, with respect to the material contained herein or for any errors or omissions that may have been made. The publisher remains neutral with regard to jurisdictional claims in published maps and institutional affiliations.

Cover illustration: Peter Lamm / GettyImages

This Palgrave Macmillan imprint is published by the registered company Springer Nature Switzerland AG.
The registered company address is: Gewerbestrasse 11, 6330 Cham, Switzerland

Acknowledgments

The editors are grateful to the Palgrave editorial team for their support and encouragement, and to anonymous reviewers whose comments have helped us reflect on, refine, and articulate our approach. This publication was supported by the Korean government through a National Research Foundation of Korea Grant to the Critical Global Studies Institute, Sogang University (Grant no. NRF-2017S1A6A3A01079727). Chapter 2 was originally published as Jie-Hyun Lim, "Triple Victimhood: On the Mnemonic Confluence of the Holocaust, Stalinist Crime, and Colonial Genocide," *Journal of Genocide Research* (April 2020), https://doi.org/10.1080/14623528.2020.1750822. It is reprinted here by the permission of Taylor and Francis Ltd. The research for Chapter 5 was begun when the authors were New Generation Scholars at the Centre for Humanities Research, University of Western Cape, and they acknowledge the University's support.

Contents

1. Introduction: Mnemonic Solidarity—Global Interventions 1
   Jie-Hyun Lim and Eve Rosenhaft

2. Postcolonial Reflections on the Mnemonic Confluence of the Holocaust, Stalinist Crimes, and Colonialism 15
   Jie-Hyun Lim

3. Europe's Melancholias: Diasporas in Contention and the Unravelings of the Postwar Settlement 45
   Eve Rosenhaft

4. What the World Owes the Comfort Women 73
   Carol Gluck

5. Eddies and Entanglements: Africa and the Global Mnemoscape 105
   Lauren van Der Rede and Aidan Erasmus

Index 131

Notes on Contributors

Aidan Erasmus is Lecturer in History at the University of the Western Cape, South Africa. He was formerly a Next Generation Scholar at the Centre for Humanities Research at the University of the Western Cape, and his doctoral research was concerned with sound, violence, and memory in South African historiographies of war. His research interests include the intersection of studies of sound, technology, and the mediation of colonial pasts and presents.

Carol Gluck is George Sansom Professor of History and Chair of the Committee on Global Thought at Columbia University, New York. She is a fellow of the American Academy of Arts and Sciences and the American Philosophical Society, former president of the Association for Asian Studies, co-chair of the Trustees Emeriti of Asia Society, and member of the Board of Directors of Japan Society. Her recent books include *Words in Motion: Toward a Global Lexicon* (2009), *Thinking with the Past: The Japanese and Modern History* (2017), and *Past Obsessions: World War Two in History and Memory* (forthcoming).

Jie-Hyun Lim is Professor of Transnational History and Director of the Critical Global Studies Institute at Sogang University, Seoul. He has published widely on nationalism and Marxism in comparison, Polish history, transnational history, and global memory. Among his recent works are the five volumes of the Palgrave series on "mass dictatorship in the twentieth century" as the series editor, 2011–2016. He is Principal Investigator of the international research project *Mnemonic Solidarity: Colonialism, War* *and Genocide in the Global Memory Space* (2017–2024). His publications on global memory include "Second World War in the Global Memory Space" in Michael Geyer and Adam Tooze eds., *Cambridge History of Second World War* (2015); "Victimhood Nationalism in Contested Memories—National Mourning and Global Accountability" in Aleida Assmann and Sebastian Conrad eds., *Memory in a Global Age: Discourses, Practices and Trajectories* (2010); "Victimhood Nationalism and History Reconciliation in East Asia," *History Compass*, vol. 8/1 (November 2009).

Eve Rosenhaft is Professor of German Historical Studies at the University of Liverpool. She has taught and published widely on aspects of German social history since the eighteenth century. Recent publications include *Black Germany: The Making and Unmaking of a Diaspora Community 1884–1960* (2013), *Slavery Hinterland. Transatlantic Slavery and Continental Europe 1680–1850* (2016), *Black German: An Afro-German Life in the Twentieth Century* (2017—a critical English edition of the memoirs of Theodor Michael), and journal articles and book chapters on the Romani genocide. Her public engagement work includes collaborations with the United States Holocaust Memorial Museum, the Imperial War Museum London, and the Wiener Holocaust Library, and developing exhibitions on the Nazi persecution of German Sinti and Roma in collaboration with German and South Korean memory practitioners.

Lauren van Der Rede is Lecturer in English at Stellenbosch University, South Africa, and a former Next Generation Scholar at the Centre for Humanities Research at the University of the Western Cape, South Africa. Her doctoral project engaged with the question of genocide through the literary and focused on its expressions in three African contexts: Rwanda, Ethiopia, and the Darfur region of Sudan. Her research elaborates this and is concerned with the intersection of genocide, cultural studies, psychoanalysis, and literature; it also offers an alternative reading of the problem of genocide centered on what it might mean to think genocide beyond the framework of the phenomenon.

List of Figures

Fig. 1.1 The tablet at the entrance to the Holocaust Education Center in Fukuyama, Hiroshima Prefecture, which is dedicated to Anne Frank's legacy, August 2012 (Jie-Hyun Lim) 1

Fig. 2.1 Descendants of the 1904–1908 genocide in Namibia at the Holocaust Memorial in Berlin 2011, on the occasion of the first repatriation of deported human remains to Namibia (Reinhard Kößler) 15

Fig. 3.1 Still from the film *Where Hands Touch* (Tantrum Films) 45

Fig. 4.1 Comfort Woman statue in Seoul (Carol Gluck) 73

Fig. 5.1 The Ethiopian Red Terror Martyrs Memorial Museum in Addis Ababa, showing a replica of the blood-filled bottle used by Mengistu to signal the start of the Red Terror, the faces of 755 individuals on the Derg "wanted list" and (1977) (reflected in the vitrine) the faces of the disappeared who are still missing (Lauren van der Rede) 105

CHAPTER 1

Introduction: Mnemonic Solidarity—Global Interventions

Jie-Hyun Lim and Eve Rosenhaft

Fig. 1.1 The tablet at the entrance to the Holocaust Education Center in Fukuyama, Hiroshima Prefecture, which is dedicated to Anne Frank's legacy, August 2012 (Jie-Hyun Lim)

J.-H. Lim
Department of History and the Critical Global Studies Institute, Sogang University, Seoul, Republic of Korea
e-mail: limjiehyun@gmail.com

© The Author(s) 2021
J.-H. Lim, E. Rosenhaft (eds.), *Mnemonic Solidarity*, Entangled Memories in the Global South,
https://doi.org/10.1007/978-3-030-57669-1_1

Abstract Lim and Rosenhaft introduce "mnemonic solidarity" as a scholarly and political program, situating it in the context of the wider project and publication series "Entangled Memories in the Global South." Their programmatic approach arises from the observation that a global memory formation has emerged since the late twentieth century, involving interchanges of various kinds between national memory cultures and structured by the terms of Holocaust memory. This development and its political implications have been addressed in various ways by scholars under the rubrics of "cosmopolitan," "multidirectional," "traveling," "prosthetic," "transnational," and "agonistic" memory, but the new field of memory studies remains Eurocentric and relatively insensitive to the double-edged character of globalized memory—the interplay between de-territorialization and re-territorialization. This volume aims to reset the agenda.

Keywords Global memory formation • Mnemonic solidarity • Global South • Territorialization • Local memory

This volume introduces a new publication series and a new emphasis in memory studies. The title of the series is *Entangled Memories in the Global South*. The term "mnemonic solidarity" which gives this book its title signals one response to the observation that historical memories have become entangled. It proposes that that entanglement invites us to rethink memory studies as a field of scholarship and also the sociocultural and political practices through which communities engage with their respective and shared histories. The central question implicit in the term "mnemonic solidarity" is how and how far it is possible to find a common ground for articulating the hurts of the past in ways that are productive for the future. The question itself is not a new one; it has been posed and answered in decades of practical and theoretical work on projects for transitional, commemorative, compensatory and restorative justice, and for historical reconciliation in particular conflict zones. The question takes on new dimensions with the emergence of the global memory formation: Historical experiences are being articulated as

E. Rosenhaft (✉)
School of Histories, Languages & Cultures, University of Liverpool,
Liverpool, UK
e-mail: dan85@liverpool.ac.uk

memory not only through interactions among the subjects of those histories but also in conversation with the historical memories of others around the world. And in those conversations the lives and voices of historical actors in the global South are increasingly heard in their own terms.

Here, we need to clarify our use of the term "global South." It does not in any sense represent a geo-positivist fixation, although it corresponds largely to the tri-continent: Asia, Africa, and Latin America. In the series, we use "North" and "South" as liquid geo-positions and historical constructs depending on the ways in which, at a given historical moment, events, questions, and actors are discursively located in global interactions.[1] At the founding conference of the Non-Alliance Movement in Bandung in 1955, for example, Japan and China belonged to the global South; this is no longer the case. Global interventions expressing mnemonic solidarity between interwar African Americans and Japanese Americans self-defining as Pacific Negroes, between the Irish in the potato famine and the Choctaw native nation after the "Trail of Tears," between Hiroshima and Auschwitz, between Muslim women victims of sexual violence in former Yugoslavia and East Asian comfort women witnessing in the transpacific space have taken place in the Northern hemisphere. But we include these interactions among "entangled memories in the Global South" because they represent suppressed voices and memories which have become to be heard with the emergence of the global memory formation. The essays in this volume explore the dimensions and implications of that global memory formation from a variety of disciplinary and regional perspectives. The authors, representing two generations of scholars, base their reflections on their study of particular histories and memory formations and also on experiences of active engagement in public history and commemoration.

The global memory formation of which we speak reflects the ways in which globalization has dramatically reconfigured the landscape of memory in the third millennium. The space in which collective memories take shape is no longer national but global, and memories have become entangled, reconciled, contested, conflicted, and negotiated across borders, connecting historical actors and events across time and space. "Formation"

---

[1] See Arif Dirlik, "Global South: Predicament and Promise," *The Global South* 1, no. 1 (2007): 12–23; Anne Garland Mahler, "Beyond the Color Curtain. The Metonymic Color Politics of the Tricontinental and the (New) Global South," in *The Global South Atlantic*, eds. Kerry Bystrom and Joseph R. Slaughter (New York: Fordham University Press, 2018), 99–123.

needs to be understood in this context as process rather than structure, and the process was accelerated (if not set in motion) by a particular historical moment: As Jie-Hyun Lim shows in his chapter, it was the thaw of memories that had been frozen under the restraint of Cold War ideologies that accelerated this global memory formation and gave new impetus to rewritings of the past, as suppressed memories of the Stalinist terror and Nazi collaboration in Eastern Europe joined new articulations of colonial trauma in the tri-continent of Africa, Asia, and Latin America.

Memory is the posthumous history of history, where interventions are constantly made to rearticulate what happened in the past. In these terms, the emerging global memory formation has two defining features. The first is a complex interplay between de-territorialization and re-territorialization. Across the globe, vernacular and institutionalized memories of past traumas are being shaped in conversations both within and across national, regional, and continental borders. Collective memories shaped in specific local, regional, or national contexts have become interwoven with one another through processes and practices of translation, cross-referencing, adaptive imagination, unilateral "re-purposing" and active dialogue, as well as competition. Almost without exception, the global South tends to create its own mnemoscape through the dynamics of comparison, cross-referencing, juxtaposition to and repulsion from the Holocaust in the global North. Many memory activists in the global South have adopted these practices as a deliberate tactic for marking out their own position in the global memory formation. And in fact testimony to and memories of human rights abuses in the global South have attracted the attention of the global public sphere largely when and as they became more interactive or entangled with the Holocaust as the ethical norm of memories. There is a degree of randomness in the way in which the remembrance of transatlantic slavery, the Nanjing massacre, the atomic bombing of Hiroshima and Nagasaki, and even the comfort women have adopted the language of Holocaust. But as Eve Rosenhaft's analysis of Black Holocaust fictions proposes, that discursive nexus has an imaginative power that reflects an authentic de-territorialization—of the tools or terms of memory, at least.

At the same time, though, the global memory formation has contributed to re-territorializing the mnemoscape by providing a new frame for heightened competition among the parties to contending national memories. Perhaps the best example of this is the way in which the globalization of Holocaust discourse has been accompanied by its appropriation in political conflicts within and between nation-states. The results of such juxtapositions can be simply scandalous. In Eastern Europe post-Communist states have nationalized Holocaust remembrance to justify a resurgent old-fashioned ethnic nationalism and provide a screen memory that obscures their own war crimes. Even among Europeans for whom the Second World War and the Holocaust are, after all, part of their local memory, the dimensions of the claims to victimhood that can be made in terms of Holocaust are practically kaleidoscopic, showing new complications as each national trauma enters into the conversation. It is disturbing, for example, to witness the efforts of the "Jasenovac Committee of the Synod of Bishops of the Serbian Orthodox Church" since the end of the Balkan civil wars to rehabilitate the Serbian-Chetnik fascists as concentration camp victims—in close collaboration with the World Holocaust Remembrance Center at Yad Vashem.[2]

This is the first ground on which the project represented by this volume responds to established currents in memory studies: The perception that key components of cultural memory—identificatory narratives about the past generated in one place or by one mnemonic community[3]—can be and have been appropriated by cultural and political actors outside that community has generated some key terms in the developing field of memory studies. At the beginning of the twenty-first century, Daniel Levy and Natan Sznaider identified a formation of "cosmopolitan memory" in the global circulation of Holocaust discourse.[4] In 2009, Michael Rothberg introduced the term "multidirectional memory" to characterize the overlaps and exchanges between Holocaust and (post)colonial memory.[5] Astrid Erll's reflections on the future of memory studies in the light of the manifest porousness of the nation-state "container" led her by way of "transcultural memory" to the influential coinage "traveling memory."[6] And the concept of "prosthetic memory" proposed by Alison Landsberg was essentially an answer to the question of how members of one mnemonic community can internalize the "memories" of another.

---

[2] Jovan Byford, "When I Say 'the Holocaust' I Mean 'Jasenovac': Remembrance of the Holocaust in contemporary Serbia," *East European Jewish Affairs* 37, no. 1 (2007): 51–74.

[3] The earliest deployment of the term is by Eliatar Zerubavel, "Social Memories: Steps to a Sociology of the Past," *Qualitative Sociology* 19, no. 3 (1996): 283–99 (here 289–91).

[4] Daniel Levy and Natan Sznaider, "Memory Unbound: The Holocaust and the Formation of Cosmopolitan Memory," *European Journal of Social Theory* 5, no. 1 (2002): 87–106; Idem., *The Holocaust and Memory in the Global Age*, trans. Assenka Oksilloff (Philadelphia: Temple University Press, 2006).

[5] Michael Rothberg, *Multidirectional Memory: Remembering the Holocaust in the Age of Decolonization* (Stanford: Stanford University Press, 2009).

[6] Astrid Erll, "Travelling Memory," *Parallax* 17, no. 4 (2011): 4–18.

Although it emerged from a study of American memory cultures, Landsberg's proposition rested on observations about global transformations in the conditions for memory, notably in the technologies through which experience is communicated.[7] The investigation of these dynamics has also been carried out under the rubric "transnational memory."[8]

The mnemonic solidarity project builds on the insights and methods of all of those scholars, but it starts from an acute awareness that the global memory space is a double-edged formation which promotes the de-territorialization and re-territorialization of remembrance simultaneously. Our concern is less with the traces of cosmopolitan memory than with continuing challenges to productive interchange between communities of memory. The forms of selective remembering that we call re-territorialization need to be anatomized and critiqued before we can move on to construct genuinely usable narratives of the pasts we share. These developments call for a program of critical rethinking which is both scholarly and political: How have particular memories and memory practices emerged out of particular historical experiences, how have they come to be appropriated as official or cultural memory or for deployment in civil and international conflicts, and what specific role does transnational exchange—the entanglement of memories—play in the formation of memory and memory practices?

Those earlier models took as their starting point questions of Holocaust memory. Reflections on how, where, when, and by whom that epochal moment in European history has been remembered have been foundational for the field of memory studies since the 1970s. Mainstream studies have built on theoretical foundations laid in the European sociological tradition and persistently focused on the European and American experiences.[9] This leads us to the second feature of the new global memory

---

[7] Alison Landsberg, *Prosthetic Memory. The Transformation of American Remembrance in the Age of Mass Culture* (New York: Columbia University Press, 2004).

[8] Chiara de Cesari and Ann Rigney, eds., *Transnational Memory: Circulation, Articulation, Scales* (Berlin and Boston: de Gruyter, 2014).

[9] Reference here is to the work of Maurice Halbwachs in the 1920s, as critiqued and elaborated by Jan and Aleida Assmann in the 1990s: Maurice Halbwachs, *On Collective Memory*, ed. and trans. Lewis A. Coser (Chicago: University of Chicago Press, 1992); Jan Assmann, "Collective Memory and Cultural Identity," *New German Critique* 65 (1995): 125-33; Aleida Assmann, *Cultural Memory and Western Civilization: Functions, Media, Archives* (Cambridge: Cambridge University Press, 2011) (originally published in German in 1999). For a recent critique of the Western-centrism of memory studies, see Hunmi Lee et al., "Conference Report: The Third Annual Conference of the Memory Studies Association in

formation that this volume addresses and which is at the core of its underlying rationale: Even as the pull of the European (Holocaust) experience continues to be powerful in global articulations of trauma, that experience is being increasingly de-centered. That same post-Cold War thaw that released suppressed memories of Stalinist terror and Nazi collaboration in Eastern Europe presaged new articulations of the violence of colonialism and neo-imperialism in other parts of the world. The rhythms and outcomes of these articulations were not uniform. In Latin America's Southern Cone, for example, the 1990s democratization was followed by an initial closing down of public discussion of Pinochet's dictatorship in Chile, while Argentina, whose dictatorship had ended a decade earlier, experienced a generational shift from the preoccupation with justice to concerns with memory.[10] In general, though, memorial practices and the critical study of them have increasingly partaken of international conversations in which scholars and activists from the global South have taken a lead. New work in this area reflects on the utility and capacity of both new technologies and repurposed everyday practices to articulate identities and empower activists at the regional level, exploring the paradoxes of re-territorialization through transnational media.[11]

This opening up has also led to new, non-hierarchical appreciations of the comparability of historical traumas. The Holocaust is ceasing to be the model of which other traumas were versions, and has become subject to postcolonial readings itself. These locate the Holocaust in the history of global colonialism, elaborating its place in a continuous development beginning (for Germany) with genocidal campaigns in German Africa and situating the German invasion and occupation of the Slavic East firmly in

Madrid, 2019," accessed November 11, 2020, http://cgsi.ac/bbs/board.php?bo_table=eng_e_Pub&wr_id=6.

[10] Eugenia Allier Montaño and Emilio A. Crenzel, eds., *The Struggle for Memory in Latin America. Recent History and Political Violence* (Basingstoke: Palgrave Macmillan, 2015).

[11] Claire Taylor and Thea Pitman, "Conclusion: Latin American Identity and Cyberspace," in *Latin American Cybercultures and Cyberliterature*, eds. Claire Taylor and Thea Pitman (Liverpool: Liverpool University Press, 2007), 263–67; Claire Taylor, *Place and Politics in Latin American Digital Culture. Location and Latin American Net Art* (New York: Routledge, 2014); Tania Pérez-Bustos, Eliana Sánchez-Aldana and Alexandra Chocontá-Piraquive, "Textile Material Metaphors to Describe Feminist Textile Activisms: From Threading Yarn, to Knitting, to Weaving Politics," *TEXTILE* 17, no. 4 (2019): 368–77; Thi Ry Duong, Edward Little and Steven High, eds., *Remembering Mass Violence: Oral History, New Media and Performance* (Toronto: University of Toronto Press, 2014). We regret that it was not possible to include a contribution from Latin America in this volume.

the European colonialist tradition. In Chap. 2, Jie-Hyun Lim elaborates this re-visioning of the Holocaust and some of the ways in which this new formation is manifested in public discourse.

Equally significant is the audibility of new actors—the global South—in the global memory formation. As Eve Rosenhaft proposes in her anatomy of "Europe's melancholias," people voicing the colonial and postcolonial experience from positions *within* the global North are now part of conversations about how past and present connect. Their perspectives on the Holocaust and its lessons, brought into contention with received narratives in a moment of political crisis, mark a mnemonic moment which is arguably as much post-Holocaust and post-postwar[12] as it is postcolonial and (surprisingly) postimperial. Global perspectives open up new temporalities, which in turn make us newly attentive to what has been forgotten or suppressed in the construction of memories.

Carol Gluck's meticulous account of how the East Asian comfort woman came to be a new global icon for historical trauma and accountability draws together key elements of the global memory formation. It exposes the importance of particular conjunctures—temporal moments—in the public understanding and speakability of human rights and war crimes. Central to the story is, of course, the global visibility of the East Asian experience of war and the entry of East Asian (women) actors into transnational mnemonic conversations. As Jie-Hyun Lim also intimates, memory developments in East Asia are in important ways fundamental to the global memory formation. Not only has the western Pacific rim been the site of intense memory conflicts arising out of the complex imperial, colonial, and postcolonial relationships among China, Japan, and Korea, but patterns of memory politics there have been very much informed by discourses of victimhood and responsibility that originated in the West. At any rate, this is how things look through the lens of Western scholarship.

If the first three substantive chapters in this volume map out some fairly familiar territory in the global mnemonic landscape, then, they also point in the direction of new themes and questions that are foundational for the mnemonic solidarity project. One of these is how the field of memory

---

[12] In the light of the developments explored in this volume, there is some irony in the observation with which Tony Judt introduced the coda to his 2005 study of Europe's successful reconstruction based on "selective forgetting": "As Europe prepares to leave World War Two behind … the recovered memory of Europe's dead Jews has become the very definition and guarantee of the continent's restored humanity." Tony Judt, *Postwar. A History of Europe since 1945* (London: Heinemann, 2005), 804.

studies itself may change as experiential perspectives and scholarly voices from Africa, Asia, and Latin America enter into the discussion—or, more radically, when we take them as our starting point. A first step here will be to take them seriously in their own terms, articulating, for example, what distinguishes East Asian memory regimes and the preconditions for memory practices *as well as* how they have appropriated Western models of "memory contest." For example, Carol Gluck reminds us that "the geopolitical postwar era in East Asia and Eastern Europe really began only after 1989."[13]

In Chap. 5, Lauren van der Rede and Aidan Erasmus invite us to take "Africa" on its own terms. Mainstream memory studies that focus on Africa have begun with institutions and practices prompted by interventions from diasporic and international agencies (the memorialization of transatlantic slavery), literary mediations in forms marketable to European and American audiences, or post-conflict and post-genocide issues of justice and representation drawing on international models and comparisons.[14] (A notable exception here is South Africa, where the injustices of apartheid were the object of global interventions before they became the subject of memory and both scholars and activists have historically operated transnationally—often representing the global South in the global North and vice versa.) Examining the cases of Ethiopia and South Africa, van der Rede and Erasmus provocatively characterize Africa as a "disobedient object" of memory studies, posing a series of radical challenges to the terms and methods of the field. At the empirical level, they point out how these cases inflect our Europe-centered models of trauma and memory. In the Ethiopian context, the forensic vocabulary introduced by post-Holocaust human rights law and discourse have been redefined in the

---

[13] See also Sheila Miyoshi Jager and Rana Mitter, "Introduction: Re-Envisioning Asia Past and Present," in *Ruptured Histories: War, Memory, and the Post-Cold War in Asia*, eds. Sheila Miyoshi Jager and Rana Mitter (Cambridge MA: Harvard University Press, 2007), 1–14. Questions of the regional particularities of the East Asian memory wars and possible approaches to reconciliation are also explored in *Northeast Asia's Difficult Past. Essays in Collective Memory*, eds. Mikyoung Kim and Barry Schwartz (Basingstoke: Palgrave Macmillan, 2010) and *East Asia beyond the History Wars. Confronting the Ghosts of Violence*, eds. Tessa Morris-Suzuki et al. (Oxford and New York: Routledge, 2013).

[14] Marie-Aude Fouéréa and Lotte Hughes, "Heritage and memory in East Africa today: a review of recent developments in cultural heritage research and memory studies," *Azania: Archaeological Research in Africa* 50 (2015): 542–58; Erica L. Johnson and Éloïse Brezault, eds., *Memory as Colonial Capital. Cross-Cultural Encounters in French and English* (Cham: Palgrave Macmillan, 2017).

legislative negotiation between "genocide" and "terror." In South Africa, the institutions and mentality that underpinned the apartheid system can be seen as resting in turn on a mnemonic infrastructure in which colonial hybridity and the identity of a nation in arms were entangled in very particular ways. Beyond this, positing Africa "not as a cartographic and geological location but as a concept and methodology," van der Rede and Erasmus challenge the liberal universalism implicit in the problematics of memory studies (and indeed in the notion of mnemonic solidarity) with an insistence on hearing/listening rather than speaking that draws on postcolonial theory and the new methods of sound studies. Mnemonic solidarity retains more than heuristic power as a normative real, but it is precisely the ways in which the de-centering of global North perspectives tests it to its limit that constitute the intellectual promise of a genuinely globalized memory studies.

One thing that is at issue in van der Rede and Erasmus' critique of liberal universalism is the obligation to speak which the emphasis on witnessing in Holocaust-informed memory studies places on the subjects of memory. This addresses the second key move in the mnemonic solidarity project: critical attention to specific actors and material processes. Who are the rememberers and what are they able to say? In memory studies as in other disciplines that employ the language of globalization, there is a danger that "territorialization" and its variants come to denote disembodied forces.[15] Our model of global memory formation is a dynamic one; far from being a simple piling-up of individual national memories, it regulates and stimulates national remembrance by co-figuring national memories—most obviously, in the self- and other-identities of perpetrator and victim nations. That formation depends in turn on the internal dynamics of national and local memory communities. Even if we fix our attention at the level of the national, the analysis of re-territorialization needs to take into account the mechanisms through which official memory regimes selectively appropriate, pre-empt and silence vernacular memory. But of course there are contests, too, among and within "grass-roots" memory communities, most acute among survivors of political repression and genocide. And memory communities themselves are subject to being

---

[15] See, for example, the critique by Stef Jansen and Staffan Löfving cited by Chiara de Cesari and Ann Rigney in their introduction to *Transnational Memory* (1–25, here 13), and the emphasis that that volume places on concrete, actor-led processes of articulation and circulation and the conditioning element of "scale."

reshaped and fractured through temporal processes of generational and demographic change, such as Eve Rosenhaft explores in Chap. 3.

This calls for caution. Acknowledging the agency and eliciting the voices of subaltern and marginalized historical actors, irrespective of where they were positioned in moments of historical trauma (whether as "victims," "perpetrators," or "bystanders"), are essential to the democratization of both narratives and resources that is part of the mnemonic solidarity project. But we need to be alert to ambivalences at the vernacular level, too. Speech may prove pointless and dialogue incapable of generating solidarity.[16] The tendency of the global memory formation to enable conversations between local memory communities is apparent in new forms of transnational memory activism, like the multiple border-crossings of the South Korean comfort woman statue discussed here in the chapters by Jie-Hyun Lim and Carol Gluck. But the popularization of national victimhood narratives and the mobilization of grass-roots actors to defend them in acts of performative nationalism, such as we see in the case of the comfort women, bespeaks the double-edged quality of memory formation at this level.[17]

Attention to the possibilities for making memory "from below" raises the question of what tools the memory makers have available: the material, institutional, and cultural conditions for the construction of vernacular memories and their articulation in and with national and global conversations. These questions are sometimes answered by giving attention to actors and events at the very local level, and this is a frontier of research whose importance we want to signal although it is not represented elsewhere in the present volume. On the one hand, locality itself is an important determinant of identity and an object of memory. The neighborhood around the Bataclan nightclub in Paris, site of a terrorist attack in November 2015, and the South Korean city of Gwangju, subject

---

[16] In memory studies, the power of dialogic confrontation between contending memories is being explored in discussions of "agonistic memory": Anna Cento Bull and Hans Lauge Hansen, "On Agonistic Memory," *Memory Studies* 9, no. 4 (2016): 390–404; Cristian Cercel, "The Military History Museum in Dresden: Between Forum and Temple," *History & Memory* 30, no. 1 (2018): 3–39.

[17] On the performative as a negotiation of popular and institutional visions of nation, see Homi Babha, "DissemiNation: Time, narrative and the margins of the modern nation," in idem., *The Location of Culture* (London: Routledge, 1994), 199–244 (here 210–17). See also Jie-Hyun Lim, "Transnational Memory Activism and Performative Nationalism," in *Handbook of Memory Activism*, eds. Jenny Wüstenberg et al. (forthcoming 2021).

to violent repression of a democracy movement in 1980, provide examples of the power of local memory, though with notable differences.[18] In the case of cities, what is remembered locally is often the struggle to retain the physical fabric of memory itself: the visible traces of a community. This is well represented in protests against redevelopment which articulate the nexus between identity and the configuration of urban space—examples of what Edward S. Casey calls "place memory" and of Andreas Huyssen's "urban imaginary." These forms of memory are haunted by the global, as resistance has often adopted the voice of nostalgia for neighborhood pasts characterized by cosmopolitan values and ethnic and social diversity.[19]

And there are other ways in which "glocal," that coinage of the 1990s, is relevant to questions of memory and mnemonic solidarity. Where most of the contributions to this volume refer to the traumas of war and genocide, "rebel cities" typically articulate the material and psychological traumas incurred by neoliberalism at the intersection of aesthetics and everyday life—where the city itself is a victim of global capital flows that drive the privatization and homogenization of urban space.[20] Per contra, in the form of housing activism, urban memory movements have acquired global networks and vocabularies.[21] It is also the case that some icons of trauma which circulate globally have very particular associations for the memory communities in the places where the event took place—associations shaped by pre-existing discourses of local identity. An example of this is the 2001

---

[18] Sarah Gensburger, *Memory on My Doorstep: Chronicles of the Bataclan Neighborhood, Paris 2015–2016*, trans. Katharine Throssell (Leuven: Leuven University Press, 2019); Linda S. Lewis, *Laying Claim to the Memory of May: A Look Back at the 1980 Kwangju Uprising* (Honolulu: University of Hawai'i Press, 2002), especially 135–51 on the simultaneous consolidation of a local identity around the trauma and efforts to insert the commemoration in the global human rights program.

[19] Edward S. Casey, *Remembering. A Phenomenological Study* (Bloomington: Indiana University Press, 2000), 181–215; Andreas Huyssen, "Introduction," in *Other Cities, Other Worlds*, ed. Andreas Huyssen (Durham NC: Duke University Press, 2008), 1–23; Dolores Hayden, *The Power of Place: Urban Landscapes as Public History* (Cambridge MA: MIT Press, 1995), 44–81; Yuan Yao and Rongbin Han, "Challenging, but not Trouble-Making: cultural elites in China's urban heritage preservation," *Journal of Contemporary China* 25, no. 98 (2016): 292–306; Martin Zebracki, "Urban preservation and the queerying spaces of (un)remembering: Memorial landscapes of the Miami Beach art deco historic district," *Urban Studies* 55, no. 10 (2018): 2261–85.

[20] Cf David Harvey, *Rebel Cities. From the Right to the City to the Urban Revolution* (London: Verso, 2012).

[21] Katia Valenzuela-Fuentes, Dominika V. Polanska and Anne Kaun, "The right to housing in theory and in practice: going beyond the West," *Interface* 9, no. 1 (2017): 359–67.

attack on the World Trade Center, whose identificatory power and mnemonic complexities for New Yorkers are being evoked by the city's experience of the coronavirus pandemic as this volume goes to press.[22] It is at the local level, too, that insurgent memories arise out of everyday hurts. Formulated as demands for justice that expose structural inequalities in democratic societies and reinforced in commemorations that enact counter-national identities, these, too, can now go global. Here, the editors of this volume cannot fail to mention the solidary encounters between the Liverpool families of the victims of the 1989 Hillsborough Disaster and those of the people (mainly teenagers) who drowned in the sinking of the Sewol Ferry off the South Korean coast in 2014.[23] Theirs are also voices of a global South.

---

[22] Setha M. Low, "The Memorialization of September 11: Dominant and Local Discourses on the Rebuilding of the World Trade Center Site," *American Ethnologist* 31, no. 3 (2004): 326–39; Simon Stow, "From Upper Canal to Lower Manhattan: Memorialization and the Politics of Loss," *Perspectives on Politics* 10, no. 3 (2012), 687–700.

[23] "Sewol and Hillsborough: families see common threads in tragedy," *Hankyoreh*, May 16, 2016, http://english.hani.co.kr/arti/english_edition/e_international/743734.html. The meeting was part of a European tour by the Sewol families in which they met with the families of victims of the 1994 sinking of the MS Estonia and of the Paris terror attacks: "Families of Sewol Ferry Victims Meet with Families of Hillsborough and MS Estonia Disaster Victims," accessed May 14, 2020, https://rememberingsewoluk.files.wordpress.com/2016/05/20160430_pressrelease_engl.pdf.

Open Access This chapter is licensed under the terms of the Creative Commons Attribution 4.0 International License (http://creativecommons.org/licenses/by/4.0/), which permits use, sharing, adaptation, distribution and reproduction in any medium or format, as long as you give appropriate credit to the original author(s) and the source, provide a link to the Creative Commons licence and indicate if changes were made.

The images or other third party material in this chapter are included in the chapter's Creative Commons licence, unless indicated otherwise in a credit line to the material. If material is not included in the chapter's Creative Commons licence and your intended use is not permitted by statutory regulation or exceeds the permitted use, you will need to obtain permission directly from the copyright holder.

CHAPTER 2

Postcolonial Reflections on the Mnemonic Confluence of the Holocaust, Stalinist Crimes, and Colonialism

Jie-Hyun Lim

Fig. 2.1 Descendants of the 1904–1908 genocide in Namibia at the Holocaust Memorial in Berlin 2011, on the occasion of the first repatriation of deported human remains to Namibia (Reinhard Kößler)

© The Author(s) 2021
J.-H. Lim, E. Rosenhaft (eds.), *Mnemonic Solidarity*, Entangled Memories in the Global South,
https://doi.org/10.1007/978-3-030-57669-1_2

Abstract Lim sets out the origins and progress of the mnemonic confluence of three historical traumas—the Holocaust, the crimes of colonialism, and Stalinist terror. He traces this process back to the "thaw" in memory cultures precipitated by the end of socialism after 1989, and adopts a postcolonial perspective to analyze how victimhood memories arising out of these experiences have become entangled globally. Against the flat model of the cosmopolitanization of the Holocaust, Lim argues for the non-hierarchical comparability of historical traumas. He concludes by proposing "critical relativization" and "radical juxtaposition" as ways of de-hegemonizing and de-centering universal memories and deconstructing mnemonic nationalism.

Keywords Global memory formation • Holocaust • Stalinism • Genocide • Postcolonialism • Critical relativization • Radical juxtaposition

Victimhood Claims at the Thaw of Cold War Memory

One of the salient features of postwar global memory formation is that the Holocaust has provided a memory template for historical traumas everywhere.[1] American slavery, the genocide of the indigenous nations of the New World, countless colonial atrocities in the global South, the Japanese A-bomb victims, the Nanjing Massacre, American war crimes in Vietnam, and the Korean comfort women (victims of military sexual slavery) are commemorated in terms drawn from the vocabulary of Holocaust memory. In Central and Eastern Europe, the painful memories of the Allied bombing and *Vertreibung* in Germany, the mass killing and enslavement of the Slavs in "Germany's Wild East," and the Ukrainian *Holodomor* and

---

[1] Daniel Levy and Natan Sznaider, *The Holocaust and Memory in the Global Age*, trans. Assenka Oksiloff (Philadelphia: Temple University Press, 2006).

J.-H. Lim (✉)
Department of History and the Critical Global Studies Institute,
Sogang University, Seoul, Republic of Korea
e-mail: limjiehyun@gmail.com

other Stalinist crimes have invoked the memory of Holocaust.[2] But Daniel Levy and Natan Sznaider's remark that, by transposing Holocaust memory onto memories of other genocides, "*Never again Auschwitz* provided the foundation for emerging cosmopolitan memories" is both right and wrong.[3] In the fifteen years since their book was written, it has become clear that Holocaust discourse is increasingly providing the mnemonic leverage for the re-territorialization and nationalization of collective memory.

Holocaust memory has been instrumentalized, vulgarized, and abused. Through the narcissistic identification with Jewish suffering, postcommunist politics in Eastern Europe nationalized Holocaust remembrance to justify a resurgent old-fashioned ethnic nationalism and activate a screen memory to cover up their own war crimes.[4] Also, one cannot but to see an inherent contradiction between the global ubiquity of the Holocaust and its supposed uniqueness. This chapter scrutinizes the mnemonic confluence and entanglements of three historical traumas—the Holocaust, colonial genocide, and Stalinist terror—in the global memory space. In particular, it explores the ways in which memories of those events have been deployed to underpin the claims of whole polities (nation-states) to the status of victim and to the material and ethical entitlements arising from that status. As these claims have become entangled in

[2] It is not my purpose here to assess the objective force of historical comparisons/analogies, a theme which has also, of course, been present in recent political theory and historiography. See, for example, Giorgio Agamben, *Homo Sacer: Sovereign Power and Bare Life*, trans. Daniel Heller-Roazen (Stanford: Stanford University Press, 1998); A. Dirk Moses, "Conceptual Blockages and Definitional Dilemmas in the 'Racial Century': Genocides of Indigenous Peoples and the Holocaust," *Patterns of Prejudice* 36, no. 4 (2020): 7–36; Jan Burzlaff, "The Holocaust and Slavery? Working Towards A Comparative History of Genocide and Mass Violence," *Journal of Genocide Research* (2020), https://doi.org/10.108 0/14623528.2020.1718355; Steven T. Katz, "Response to Jan Burzlaff's Review of Steven T. Katz, The Holocaust and New World Slavery," *Journal of Genocide Research* (2020), https://doi.org/10.1080/14623528.2020.1718357.

[3] Daniel Levy and Natan Sznaider, "Memory Unbound: the Holocaust and the Formation of Cosmopolitan Memory," *European Journal of Social Theory* 5, no. 1 (2002): 87–106 (here 99).

[4] Lea David, "Holocaust Discourse as a Screen Memory: the Serbian Case," in *History and Politics in the Western Balkans: Changes at the Turn of the Millennium*, eds. Srdan M. Jovanovic and Veran Stancetic (Belgrade: The Center for Good Governance Studies, 2013), 64–88 (here 65, 67, 69, 71, 79); Jelena Subotić, *Yellow Star, Red Star: Holocaust Remembrance after Communism* (Ithaca: Cornell University Press, 2019), 5–11.

globalized discourse, *competition* for recognition of national grievance has intensified.

The key moment in this development came in the 1990s, as official memories frozen by the Cold War ideology began to thaw. This thaw released suppressed memories all over the world. In the former Soviet bloc, the official myths of anti-fascist struggle lost their power as screen memories,[5] and vernacular remembrance of the Stalinist terror erupted into the public sphere. At the same time, there emerged previously unspoken memories of Nazi collaboration in Eastern Europe, triggering an East European version of the *Historikerstreit* which had convulsed West Germany in the decade before the Wall came down. In the tri-continent of Asia, Africa, and Latin America, the fall of communism also signaled the release of memories of the atrocities committed by Western colonialisms. Memories of colonial genocide and anti-communist political atrocities could no longer be marginalized, because the propaganda imperative to defend Western civilization against Soviet barbarism lost its power. The colonial scars sutured by the worldwide anti-communist alliance became porous, and it became possible to articulate the hurts of colonial occupation and economic imperialism as such before a global public.

In the post-Cold War environment, the victimhood claims arising from those historical traumas become entangled, producing a global memory formation. By this I mean neither the global memory *space* as a fact or a condition, nor the simple compilation or comparative juxtaposition of separate memories within it. Formation here denotes process, and scrutiny of how this triad of victimhoods has become entangled can shed new light on the dynamics of that process in the twenty-first century. Global memory formation is in a constant state of becoming, and its outcomes depend on specific mnemonic interactions between the global template (in this case Holocaust and to a lesser extent colonialism) and local sensitivities. This chapter traces some key interactions and considers the possibilities for mnemonic solidarity they contain (and how they have been frustrated). The *Historikerstreit* of the 1980s introduced the term "relativization" to characterize arguments that juxtaposed the crimes of the Nazis and Bolshevik terror with the purpose of diminishing the enormity of the Holocaust and "moving beyond" West Germany's public culture of

---

[5] On the origins and uses of the term "screen memory," see Michael Rothberg, *Multidirectional Memory: Remembering the Holocaust in the Age of Decolonization* (Stanford: Stanford University Press, 2009), 12–16.

historical self-reflection and apology. This chapter ends by affirming the value of remembering historical traumas together and in relation to one another, but calls for a critical approach that resists political instrumentalization and the temptation to create hierarchies of victimhood by deploying strategies of "critical relativization" and "radical juxtaposition."

(Post)Colonial and Holocaust Identities: Alibis and Alliances

Amid the refugee crisis that shook Europe in September 2015, a debate broke out among Polish historians on how to interpret Eastern European apathy or even antipathy toward Islamic refugees. *Gazeta Wyborcza*'s report about remarks by Jan Gross sparked the controversy. In an article in *Die Welt*, he had claimed that East European hostility toward the refugees originated in a failure to come to terms with the Holocaust past. Gross argued that critical reflection on Eastern Europeans' complicity in the murder of the Jews might have resulted in more empathy with refugees. He asserted that Poles even murdered more Jews than Germans, challenging the myth of the unity of the resistance to German occupation.[6] Since Gross has been arguing for Polish complicity in the Holocaust since the publication of *Neighbors* in 2000, his article in *Die Welt* is not very surprising.

Even so, Gross's point is intriguing. He was suggesting that Eastern European attitudes to Islamic refugees reflect a "wrong" memory practice—challenging the relativization or marginalization of the Holocaust in the Polish mnemoscape. In Eastern Europe, Nazism and communism figure as twin evils in post-Communist memory, with communism widely regarded as the greater evil in its duration, intensity, and temporal proximity. Particularly in the Baltics and Poland, the Holocaust has been regarded as peripheral to national suffering under Stalinist oppression.[7] Gross's argument targeted the relativization or marginalization of the Holocaust in the Polish mnemoscape.

---

[6] Bartosz T. Wieliński, "'Polska nie chce uchodźców, bo nie rozliczyła się ze zbrodni na Żydach.' Oburzenie po tekście Grossa," *Wyborcza.pl*, September 15, 2015, http://wyborcza.pl/1,75968,18817369,skandalista-gross.html#ixzz420HIHBty.

[7] Siobhan Kattago, "Agreeing to Disagree on the Legacies of Recent History Memory, Pluralism and Europe after 1989," *European Journal of Social Theory* 12, no. 3 (2009): 375–95 (here 382); Martin Evans, "Memories, Monuments, Histories: the re-thinking of the Second World War since 1989," *National Identities* 8, no. 4 (2006): 317–48 (here 320).

Polish historians Marcin Zaremba and Aleksander Smolar came to the defense of the Poles by pointing to the absence of a colonial past in Poland and other Eastern European countries. Unlike Western Europeans (including Germans), who have historical experience of ruling over colonial subjects, they argued, Poles have had no chance to become familiar with people of different cultures, religions, and/or race. Poland has never been a colonial power that had to deal with a native Other.[8] Paradoxically, the discursive connectivity of anti-Semitism and Islamophobia is no secret in contemporary Poland, as manifested in the widespread joke that "we are ready to accept refugees because we have always had concentration camps."[9] But the implication of Zaremba and Smolar's argument was a specifically anti-colonial indictment: "You are guilty of colonialism, but we are innocent. So the refugee problem belongs to you." From the postcolonial viewpoint, we can say that their anti-colonial rhetoric bespeaks the ambivalence of Polish Orientalism: the aspiration to be included into Western Europe while orientalizing the imagined internal other within Poland.

A cursory look at the history of Poland's partition by Russia, Austria, and Prussia, the trajectories of national irredentism, and the suffering of the Polish nation at large may give credence to the notion of Poland's colonial innocence. But Poland was the colonizer against the Lithuanian and Ukrainian neighbors in the *kresy* (borderland) at the same time as German settlers were colonizing Poland. Treated as a hinterland, the first model of underdevelopment, and "a neglected suburb of Europe," Poles have never been free of the West's "intellectual project of demi-Orientalization."[10] But they have responded by developing disrespectful attitudes toward other "more eastern" and "less western" Slavic neighbors. And this reflects Poland's status as subaltern empire: subaltern *vis-à-*

---

[8] Wieliński, "'Polska nie chce uchodźców, bo nie rozliczyła się ze zbrodni na Żydach.'"; Aleksander Smolar, "Smolar: Gross szokuje," *Wyborcza.pl*, September 16, 2015, http://wyborcza.pl/1,75968,18824173,smolar-gross-szokuje.html.

[9] Marek Rymsza, "Dyskusja: czy to nasza sprawa?" *Więź* 4, no. 662 (2015): 36–46 (here 42).

[10] Lucy Mably et al., "'Other' Posts in 'Other' Places: Poland through a Postcolonial Lens?" *Sociology* 50, no. 1 (2016): 60–76 (here 66); Larry Wolff, *Inventing Eastern Europe: The Map of Civilization on the Mind of the Enlightenment* (Stanford: Stanford University Press, 1994), 9; Jerzy Jedlicki, *A Suburb of Europe: Nineteenth-Century Polish Approaches to Western Civilization* (Budapest: Central European University Press. 1999), xiii.

vis Germany and the "West," yet fully incorporated in the global structure of domination as the repressive local agent of the great powers.[11] It is this complex situation that fueled Vladimir Putin's anti-Polish campaign in the run-up to the 75th anniversary of the liberation of Auschwitz in 2020. Poland's ambivalent position under Nazi occupation provided the excuse for Putin to whitewash Stalin's handshake with Hitler and erase the first two years of World War II.[12]

Internal colonialism, too, was entirely characteristic of Poland's Second Republic (1918–1939). This was a multi-ethnic state, where ethnic Poles formed only about 68.9% of the whole population. The rest were Ukrainians, Jews, Belorussians, Germans, and others. Polish nationalists regretted that it remained "not a nation-state but a state of nationalities."[13] Józef Piłsudski's *Sanacja* regime responded to the demands of ethnic minorities by setting up the internment camp at Bereza Kartuska in 1934. Internal colonialism, demi-Orientalism against the *kresy* (borderlands) and Eastern Slavic neighbors, and the fusion of anti-Semitism and anti-Bolshevism in official discourse colluded rhetorically with the anti-Slavic and anti-Semitic propaganda that would mark the Nazi colonial occupation of Poland itself. Polish nationalism was no exception to the "ambivalent hybrid" of desire and resentment typical of subaltern imperialists.

What Poland lacks is not colonial experience, but postcolonial criticism toward internal colonialism. In the communist era, hundreds of thousands of contract workers from Asia and Africa flowed into East Germany, Poland, Czechoslovakia, and the Baltic Soviet republics. This evidences the existence of a "global socialist ecumene" which promoted

---

[11] For Subaltern Empire, see Viatcheslav Morozov, "Subaltern Empire? Toward a Postcolonial Approach to Russian Foreign Policy," *Problems of Post-Communism* 60, no. 6 (2013): 16–28; Jordan Sand, "Subaltern Imperialists: The New Historiography of the Japanese Empire," *Past and Present*, no. 225 (November 2014): 273–88.

[12] Anshel Pfeffer, "In New Battle Over Auschwitz Legacy, Poland Falls Victim to Holocaust Geopolitics," *Haaretz*, January 22, 2020, https://www.haaretz.com/israel-news/.premium-the-dirty-politics-behind-israel-s-capitulation-to-putin-s-wwii-revisionism-1.8406565/.premium-the-dirty-politics-behind-israel-s-capitulation-to-putin-s-wwii-revisionism-1.8406565; Ofer Aderet, "The Dirty Politics Behind Israel's Capitulation to Putin's WWII Revisionism," *Haaretz*, March 8, 2020, https://www.haaretz.com/israel-news/.premium-auschwitz-75-years-israel-yad-vashem-poland-victim-holocaust-geopolitics-putin-1.8432285/.premium-auschwitz-75-years-israel-yad-vashem-poland-victim-holocaust-geopolitics-putin-1.8432285.

[13] Janusz Pajewski, *Budowa Drugiej Rzeczypospolitej 1918–26* (Kraków: PAU, 1995), 164.

transnational flows of ideas, knowledge and cultural artifacts and the transnational mobility of people. And this ecumene did not come to an end even after the collapse of the communist bloc. The fact that Poland has accepted 100,000 Chechen refugees or exiles since 1996 refutes the proposition that Islamophobia is a fixed memory template in post-communist Poland. But while these numbers are impressive, the recent refugee crisis has seen a dramatic shift from empathy to apathy in the Polish attitude toward Chechens.[14]

In short, the debate over the refugee question is not a factological, but an epistemological one, in which collective guilt for anti-Semitism and colonial innocence are competing to provide the narrative template for post-communist collective memory. Gross's criticism that Polish society's hostility to Islamic refugees represents its failure to come to terms with the past of the Holocaust makes sense, but it is only partially correct. The blunt insensitivity toward them even among critical intellectuals really does bespeak the absence of postcolonial self-criticism. It is the combination of tropes that counts, though: the memory of *colonial* victimization under Nazism and Stalinism operates as a screen memory to suppress the knowledge of complicity in the Holocaust. The "*Historikerstreit po polsku*," a heated debate around Jan Błoński's seminal essay "Biedny polacy patrzą na getto" (poor Poles look at the ghetto) in 1987, followed by the reception of Jan Gross's book *Sąsiedzi* (Neighbors) in 2000, led to "a genuine moral revolution" in post-communist Poland by breaking through the anti-fascist screen memory and bringing suppressed guilt to the surface. However, even the metamorphosis of Polish self-definition from innocent victim to "Homo Jedvabnecus" after 2000 did not produce a *critical* postcolonial response. Poland is still waiting for a mnemonic confluence of the Holocaust and the postcolonial that does justice to the complexity of its wartime experiences.

Outside the realm of political rhetorics, postcolonial readings of the Holocaust have elaborated the historical continuities between German colonial genocide, the Nazis' Eastern occupation policy, and the Holocaust, helping us to situate the German invasion and occupation of the Slavic East firmly in the European colonialist tradition.[15] The *Generalplan Ost*

---

[14] See a Chechen refugee resident in Poland—Malika Abdoulvakhabova's witness: Rymsza, "Dyskusja: czy to nasza sprawa?" *Wiez* 662 (2015): 36–46 (here 36, 38, 39).

[15] Jürgen Zimmerer, "Die Geburt des Ostlandes aus dem Geiste des Kolonialismus: Die nationalsozialistische Eroberungs- und Beherrschungspolitik in (post-)kolonialer

assumed that the SS would run latifundia in the occupied territories exploiting native Slav labor until the Germans were numerous and mechanized enough to do without them. To German settlers in the occupied *Generalgouvernement*, pioneering in the East was "colonial work" like work under the African sun. As Reich Economic Minister Walter Funk wrote, "vast territories of the European East will be Europe's promising colonial land of the future."[16] By blaming Poland's backwardness on the Jewish influence, moreover, some Nazis could combine the rationale of Germany's civilizing mission with crusading anti-Semitism. In short, Nazism was an "intra-European colonialism."[17]

In Europe, there has been emotional resistance to situating Nazism and the Holocaust within the context of global colonialism. An implicit Eurocentrism insists that "the Holocaust stands out from other genocides because it was committed in the heart of civilized Europe rather than in the midst of (supposedly) primitive or barbaric societies."[18] Zygmunt Bauman anticipated this argument thirty years ago, with his warning that Holocaust-style genocide is a logical outcome not of premodern barbarity, but of Western modernity.[19] And as early as 1950 Aimé Césaire pinpointed the dilemma of Eurocentric intellectuals: "[The European bourgeois] has a Hitler inside him ... and ... what he cannot forgive Hitler for is not the *crime* in itself, the *crime against man*, it is not *the humiliation of man as such*, it is the crime against the white man, and the fact that he applied to Europe colonialist procedures which had until then been reserved exclu-

---

Perspektive," *Sozial Geschichte* 19, no. 1 (2004): 10–43; Benjamin Madley, "From Africa to Auschwitz: How German South West Africa Incubated Ideas and Methods Adopted and Developed by the Nazis in Eastern Europe," *European History Quarterly* 35, no. 3 (2005): 429–64; Enzo Traverso, *The Origins of Nazi Violence* (New York: The New Press, 2003); Robert Gerwarth and Stephan Malinowski, "Der Holocaust als kolonialer Genozid? Europäische Kolonialgewalt und nationalsozialistischer Vernichtungskrieg," *Geschichte und Gesellschaft* 33 (2007): 439–66; A. Dirk Moses, "Empire, Colony, Genocide: Keywords and the Philosophy," in *Empire, Colony, Genocide*, ed. A. Dirk Moses (New York and Oxford: Berghahn Books, 2008), 3–54.

[16] David Furber, "Near as Far in the Colonies: The Nazi Occupation of Poland," *The International History Review* 26, no. 3 (2004): 541–79 (here 541, 544, 549).

[17] Moses, "Empire, Colony, Genocide: Keywords and the Philosophy," 34.

[18] Dan Stone, "The Historiography of Genocide: Beyond 'Uniqueness' and Ethnic Competition," *Rethinking History* 8, no. 1 (2004): 127–42 (here 133).

[19] Zygmunt Bauman, *Modernity and the Holocaust* (Ithaca: Cornell University Press, 2000), xi–xii, 28, 152 and passim.

sively for the Arabs of Algeria, the 'coolies' of India, and the 'niggers' of Africa."[20] Remarkably, People's Poland published a translation of Césaire's *Discours sur le colonialisme* early in 1950—an example of how Poland's communist postcolonialism drew an analogy between the Slavic East under the Nazi occupation of the "Third Europe" and the postcolonial states of the "Third World."[21] This analogy is strikingly absent from the work of post-communist liberal historians in Poland, who still (or again) suffer the ambivalent feelings of envy, admiration, and distrust toward Western Europe which shaped the *mentalité* of the nineteenth-century intelligentsia and which bespeak the country's triple position as former colony, former colonizer, and subject to Western hegemons.

But as the case of Aimé Césaire reminds us, the perception of a family resemblance between Nazi racism and colonialism in Europe and the oppressions of (internal) colonialism and the racial state elsewhere was present in the observations of Afro-diasporic intellectuals from a very early stage. The confluence of anti-Semitism and racism can be found in W. E. B. Du Bois' memory of an incident during his trip to Galicia in 1890, when a small-gown cabman asked if Du Bois wanted to stop "Unter die Juden," in a local hotel run by a Jew. To that cabman, Du Bois, an African-American, was no different from a Jew. And the fact that Germans were more hostile to Jews than to him as a "Negro" taught him that racism is about more than color prejudice.[22] Galician Jews and African Americans were entangled that way in the late nineteenth century. Nor was Du Bois the first to recognize those entanglements. The Black Atlantic slave communities strengthened their self-esteem by seeing their oppression and their hopes through the lens of the Jewish exodus from slavery in Egypt, revaluing their suffering as a redemptive experience.[23]

Di Shklaferay, the Yiddish version of the *Uncle Tom's Cabin*, is a good example of the "return traffic" in this exchange. Ayzik-Meyer Dik adapted the novel to Jewish circumstances, making the master a Jew, and having Uncle Tom escape to freedom in Canada with the Jewish master's kind

---

[20] Aimé Césaire, *Discourse on Colonialism*, trans. J. Pinkham (New York: Monthly Review, 2000), 36.

[21] Adam F. Kola, *Socjalistyczny Postkolonializm: Rekonsolidacja pamięci* (Toruń: NCU Press, 2018), 2–3.

[22] W. E. B. Du Bois, "The Negro and the Warsaw Ghetto," in *The Oxford W. E. B. Du Bois Reader*, ed. Eric. J. Sundquist (Oxford: Oxford University Press, 1996), 470.

[23] Paul Gilroy, *The Black Atlantic: Modernity and Double Consciousness* (London: Verso, 1993), 207–8.

help. *Di Shklaferay* became a bestseller among immigrant Jews to America in the late nineteenth century. The New York Yiddish newspaper *Forverts* compared the emancipation of American slaves with the Jewish Exodus from Egypt and in 1927 urged American Jews to watch the film of *Uncle Tom's Cabin*. Radical Jews sent their children to racially integrated summer camps. The spirit of solidarity between African Americans and Jews continued in the work of the NAACP, in which many liberal and radical Jews participated. In 1952 Louis Harap, the managing editor of *Jewish Life*, invited Du Bois to a concert-meeting in "Tribute to the Warsaw Ghetto Fighters." He asked Du Bois to speak on the "significance of the ghetto fight for the Negro people in the United States today in relation to cooperation with their allies, the Jewish people and the common people of America."[24] In his speech, Du Bois spoke of recalling "the scream and shots of a race riot in Atlanta and the marching of the Ku Klux Klan" during his visit to the ruins of the Warsaw ghetto in 1949. He acknowledged that he was able to gain a "more complete understanding of the Negro problem" through a "cleared understanding of the Jewish problem in the world."[25] The swift response by African Americans to the 1948 "Genocide Convention" is another landmark. *We Charge Genocide*, a petition delivered by African-American Communists to the United Nations in 1951, invoked global awareness of the Holocaust to make a link between the crimes of the Nazis and Jim Crow America. Their action met a negative response from Raphael Lemkin, the chief proponent of the genocide concept and the UN Convention, who was fearful of losing American support.[26]

The dialogue of Blacks and Jews is also found in apartheid South Africa. For many prominent anti-apartheid activists, the diary of Anne Frank was a treasured text, with handwritten copies circulating even in the notorious Robben Island prison. In one of his public addresses as president of

---

[24] W. E. B. Du Bois, "Letter from Jewish Life to W. E. B. Du Bois, February 13, 1952," W. E. B. Du Bois Papers (MS 312) Special Collections and University Archives, University of Massachusetts Amherst Libraries, accessed March 8, 2020, http://credo.library.umass.edu/view/full/mums312-b137-i103.

[25] Du Bois, "The Negro and the Warsaw Ghetto," 471.

[26] Ann Curthoys and John Docker, "Defining Genocide," in *The Historiography of Genocide*, ed. Dan Stone (Basingstoke: Palgrave Macmillan, 2010), 9–41 (here 16–21); David Helps, "'We Charge Genocide': Revisiting Black Radicals' Appeals to the World Community," *Radical Americas* 3, no. 1 (2018): 1–24 (here 9).

post-apartheid democratic South Africa, Nelson Mandela remembered that Anne's diary had reinforced his confidence in the invincibility of the cause of freedom and justice. The anti-racist activists drew on the analogy with Nazism to characterize the apartheid system and to mobilize international support for the anti-apartheid movement as the most critical moral battle in the postwar world. The three successive exhibitions of "Nazisme in Zuid-Afrika" held in Anne Frank House in Amsterdam in the early 1970s, jointly organized by the Pluto (the Dutch-South African student group) and the Dutch Anti-Apartheid Movement, provide us with an excellent example of the interaction of postcolonial and Holocaust memory. Visitors could see the banner declaring "Nazism=Apartheid" and a life-size *papier-mâché* doll of then-Prime Minister B.J. Vorster holding a swastika.[27] Black British critic Paul Gilroy's *Black Atlantic* and *Between Camps* are nothing other than the attempt to recover this history of dialogue between Blacks and Jews. The postcolonial matters in the transatlantic nexus of memories.[28]

NAGASAKI AND AUSCHWITZ

"Stunned by the intense air of death" during his first visit to Auschwitz in 1987, Nakatani Takeshi works as a tour guide at Poland's national Auschwitz-Birkenau museum. After passing the examination for official guides, he started working there in 1997. He hopes the tour he leads can help Japanese visitors to understand "the suffering of victims and the importance and fragility of peace." But for him the museum does not prompt reflection on the East Asian wartime experience.[29] Hirano Yumie, who serves as a "keeper of memory" of the A-bomb experience in

---

[27] Shirli Gilbert, "Anne Frank in South Africa," *Holocaust and Genocide Studies* 26, no. 3 (Winter 2012): 366–93 (here 366, 374).

[28] There is not space here to explore the growing evidence for exchanges across the "Black Pacific," but see Yuichiro Onishi, "The New Negro of the Pacific: How African Americans Forged Cross-Racial Solidarity with Japan, 1917–1922," *Journal of African American History* 92, no. 2 (2007): 191–213; Bill Mullen, *Afro-Orientalism* (Minneapolis: University of Minnesota Press, 2004); Yuichiro Onishi, *Trans-Pacific Anti-racism: Afro-Asian Solidarity in twentieth-Century Black America, Japan, and Okinawa* (New York and London: New York University Press, 2013); Etsuko Taketani, *The Black Pacific Narrative: Geographic Imaginings of Race and Empire between the World Wars* (Hanover, NH: Dartmouth College Press, 2014).

[29] Toshihisha Onishi, "Auschwitz guide works to enlighten Japanese visitors," *Japan Times*, March 5, 2015, https://www.japantimes.co.jp/news/2015/03/05/national/history/auschwitz-guide-works-to-enlighten-japanese-visitors/#.WrhbWIiuyUl.

Hiroshima Peace Memorial Park, has a different approach. The City of Hiroshima launched a program for ordinary citizens to communicate the stories of A-bomb survivors (*hibakusha* in Japanese) and their desire for peace in 2012. Since then, she has visited Peru, Mongolia, and Iceland to share *hibakusha* accounts. In an interview before her visit to Poland in 2015, she said, "many Jews were killed because of racial discrimination, and innocent civilians were killed in Hiroshima. I want to convey how human rights are abused at a time of war."[30]

Two Japanese memory agents hold different, almost opposite, views on the mnemonic connectivity and historical comparability of Auschwitz and Hiroshima. If the Auschwitz tour guide sticks to the incommensurability of the Holocaust, the Hiroshima memory keeper unreservedly compares Auschwitz and Hiroshima. This difference may come from the differences in the training they received: Nakatani's training to be an Auschwitz guide combined the official memory of Poland and Israel, while Hirano's practice as a voluntary memory keeper in Hiroshima epitomizes the dominant discourse of A-bomb victimhood in Japan. The divide between those Japanese memory agents indicates the complexity of the Auschwitz-Hiroshima connection.

Nevertheless, A-bomb victims in Japan were already invoking the Holocaust in "year zero"—1945. The first sign of entanglement appeared on November 23, 1945, in Nagasaki. At a memorial mass for Catholic *hibakusha*, Nagai Takashi delivered a funeral oration to about 600 survivors holding 8000 small white crosses to represent the Catholic victims. The speech reportedly moved the whole congregation to tears.[31] The original manuscript of Nagai's funeral address reads: "The atomic bomb was originally destined for the prefectural offices at the center of Nagasaki. But because of weather conditions, the wind carried the plane north to Urakami, and the bomb exploded above the cathedral there ... we want to believe that the Urakami church was chosen not as a victim but as a pure lamb, to be slaughtered and burned on the altar of sacrifice to expiate the sins committed by humanity in the Second World War." The redemptive

---

[30] Sakiko Masuda, "'Memory Keeper' Yumie Hirano to visit Poland in May, Convey Survivors' Experiences of Atomic Bombing," *The Chugoku Shinbun*, April 18, 2018, http://www.hiroshimapeacemedia.jp/?p=59331.

[31] For this and what follows: Konishi Tetsuro, "The Original Manuscript of Takashi Nagai's Funeral Address at a Mass for the Victims of the Nagasaki Atomic Bomb," *Journal of Nagasaki University of Foreign Studies*, no. 18 (2014): 55–68.

discourse apparent in the African diaspora's invocation of the Jewish exodus reappears again in postwar Nagasaki.

Nagai went on to say, "We want to believe that only the sacrificial victim of Urakami could bring the war to an end; by this sacrifice, billions who would otherwise have fallen victims to the ravages of war have been saved." Then, Nagai picked out the word *hansai* (燔祭), the Japanese translation of the term "holocaust" from Chapter 22 of the Old Testament book of Genesis, to illustrate the sublime world-redemptive suffering of the A-bomb victims: "How noble, how splendid was that holocaust of 9 August, when flames soared up from the cathedral, dispelling the darkness of war and bringing the light of peace!" Nagai's speech is one of the earliest recorded public uses of "holocaust" in the postwar global memory space. Considering that the term was not popular even in Israel and the "West" until the late 1950s, his 1945 reference seems all the more remarkable.[32]

Nagai's use of "holocaust" was not a direct reference to Auschwitz, but it invited a comparison in some aspects at least. With its biblical semiotics, *hansai* contributed to sacralizing meaningless death into holy sacrifice to atone for the sins of humankind and contribute to universal salvation. But the sublimation of victims (*higaisha*) into sacrifices (*giseisha*) also fed a nationalist project. Political religion comes into being by conferring a holy status on earthly entities like the nation, state, class, history, and race. It binds the individual to the sacralized secular body through a code of ethical and social commandments.[33] The sacralization of the nation activates suppressed memories of suffering incurred in the national project under the aura of sacrifice.[34] In this sense, Nagai's thesis that placed Urakami

---

[32] For the earliest uses of Holocaust in the West, see Steve Friess, "When 'Holocaust' became 'The Holocaust'," *The New Republic*, May 18, 2015, https://newrepublic.com/article/121807/when-holocaust-became-holocaust See also Sean Warsch, "A 'holocaust' Becomes 'the Holocaust'," *The Jewish Magazine*, http://www.jewishmag.com/107mag/holocaustword/holocaustword.htm; Jon Petrie, "The secular word Holocaust: Scholarly myths, history, and 20th century meanings," *Journal of Genocide Research* 2, no. 1 (2000): 31–63.

[33] Emilio Gentile, "The Sacralisation of Politics: Definitions, Interpretations and Reflections on the Question of Secular Religion and Totalitarianism," *Totalitarian Movements and Political Religions* 1 (2000): 18–55.

[34] See Jie-Hyun Lim, "Victimhood Nationalism in Contested Memories-National Mourning and Global Accountability," in *Memory in a Global Age: Discourses, Practices and Trajectories*, eds. Aleida Assmann and Sebastian Conrad (Basingstoke: Palgrave Macmillan, 2010), 138–62.

Cathedral at the center of a holocaust enriched the psychological texture of Japanese victimhood nationalism.

In postwar Japan, Auschwitz and Hiroshima were frequently cited as terrible twin symbols of man-made mass death and even singled out as two archetypical examples of White racism.[35] The extensive Japanese press coverage of the Eichmann trial promoted the association of Hiroshima and Nagasaki with Holocaust. The poet and peace activist Kurihara Sadako drew a succinct analogy: "Of the world's two great holocausts, Auschwitz was a major atrocity carried out by the enemies of the victorious Allies; Hiroshima/Nagasaki was a major atrocity carried out by Allies." She even suggested that Hiroshima was worse than Auschwitz because *hibakusha* had to suffer from the after-effects of radiation exposure while Auschwitz had an end-point.[36] Rarely tainted by sporadic anti-Semitism and Holocaust denial scandals,[37] the analogy of Auschwitz and Hiroshima never disappeared from the Japanese mnemoscape.

Ran Zwigenberg has explored the intriguing case of the Hiroshima-Auschwitz Peace March. Four Japanese memory agents-cum-anti-nuclear peace activists left Hiroshima in March 1962 to participate in the commemoration of the liberation of Auschwitz on January 27, 1963. Satō Kyōtsū, a Buddhist monk and a veteran of the Japanese imperial army, led the peace pilgrimage. He declared that its aim was "to deepen the connection between these two places of utmost suffering and tragedy in World War II." On the route to Auschwitz, they visited World War II memorial sites in Vietnam, Singapore, Israel, Greece, Yugoslavia, and Hungary. This can probably be characterized as the first mnemonic pilgrimage on a global scale covering the Euro-Asian memory space, and Zwigenberg's presentation of it as an early exemplar of cosmopolitan memory is relatively persuasive.[38]

---

[35] Ian Buruma, *The Wages of Guilt: Memories of War in Germany and Japan* (New York: New York Review of Books, 2015), 92–9; John W. Dower, "An Aptitude for Being Unloved: War and Memory in Japan," in *Crimes of War: Guilt and Denial in the Twentieth Century* eds. Omer Bartov, Atina Grossmann and Mary Nolan (New York: The New Press, 2002), 226.

[36] Sadako Kurihara, "The Literature of Auschwitz and Hiroshima," *Holocaust and Genocide Studies* 7 (1993): 77–106 (here 86, 87). The Japanese original was published in 1984.

[37] Rotem Kowner, "Tokyo Recognizes Auschwitz: The Rise and Fall of Holocaust Denial in Japan, 1989–1999," *Journal of Genocide Research* 3, no. 2 (2001): 257–72 (here 257, 259, and passim).

[38] Ran Zwigenberg, "Never Again: Hiroshima, Auschwitz and the Politics of Commemoration," *Asia-Pacific Journal* 13:3, no. 1 (2015): 1–22; See also Ran Zwigenberg,

In practice, though, the Hiroshima-Auschwitz Peace March was more like a mnemonic obstacle race. First, Cold War ideology delayed its departure. The Japanese authorities refused to issue passports for the Japanese activists, on the grounds that they were displaying political bias in commemorating the crimes of Germans at Auschwitz and not the massacre committed by Soviet soldiers at Katyn. In contrast, People's Poland welcomed the Japanese peace activists, since from the perspective of the Polish communist party Hiroshima was a crime of American imperialism and the Peace March demonstrated its affinity with Nazism. *Dziennik Polski*, a Cracow newspaper, reported on the appearance of the Hiroshima peace delegates at the 1963 Auschwitz liberation commemorations. The report stressed Satō's advocacy of the A-bomb free Central Europe agenda propagated by the Polish government.[39]

But this involved an inverted memory of the Japanese empire that exposes the ambivalence of cosmopolitan memory. In this mnemoscape, Japan occupied a postcolonial rather than a postimperial position, as the "Pacific War" between Japan and the USA became just one episode in Japan's century-long struggle and defeat against the colonialism of the Western Great Powers.[40] Within this frame, Japan could remain an innocent victim in the process of coming to terms with the wartime past. And the American crime against Japanese civilians represented by the A-bomb served to reinforce this, while the misery and suffering of Japan's Taiwanese, Korean, Chinese, Vietnamese, Indonesian, Filipino, and other Asian neighbors were consigned to oblivion. The Peace March participants regarded themselves as the authentic victims and heroic pacifists until they were confronted with the accusations of the Japanese war atrocities during the pilgrimage. And despite this challenge, the pilgrims carried on.

Moreover, ethnically non-Japanese victims remained marginalized in the cosmopolitan memory that associated Hiroshima with Auschwitz. Even Oe Kenzaburo, one of the writers and intellectuals most sensitive to the minority question, confessed that he had ignored the Korean A-bomb victims in his insightful reportage on anti-nuclear pacifism and memory in

---

Hiroshima: the Origins of Global Memory Culture (Cambridge: Cambridge University Press, 2014).

[39] "Pierwszy dzień wolności…" *Dziennik Polski*, January 29, 1963.

[40] Sebastian Conrad, "The Dialectics of Remembrance: Memories of Empire in Cold War Japan," *Comparative Studies in Society and History* 56 (2014): 4–33 (here 13, 17–18).

Hiroshima.[41] The ethnocentric memory of their own victimization blocked the sensibility among many Japanese for the suffering of others under Japanese occupation. Remembering Hiroshima and Nagasaki quickly became a way of forgetting Nanjing, Bataan, comfort women, and other Japanese atrocities.[42] Rather, in interviews with *hibakusha*, reflections on the moral adequacy of the desire for revenge against Germans and Americans respectively, could evoke tirades against the vengefulness of the Koreans.[43] As James Orr puts it, Hiroshima became "an icon of Japan's past as an innocent war victim and a beacon for its future as a pacifist nation."[44] Yoneyama Lisa offers a more radical diagnosis, arguing that "the claim to posit a universal category of humanity as the subject of memorialization serves to obstruct condemnation of Japanese nationalism and ethnocentrism."[45]

One cannot but be sceptical about the "cosmopolitan memory" connecting Hiroshima and Auschwitz in the 1960s. In the death diplomacy of exchanging the ashes of unidentified victims between the two sites, for example, it vulgarized the memento mori of the genocide. Moreover, it implied the nationalist appropriation of the Holocaust on the Japanese side as well as its ideological instrumentalization on the Polish side. In the Euro-Asian space it worked as a screen memory to cover the suffering of those subject to Japanese colonialism—a function similarly fulfilled by an obsessive interest in Anne Frank. Almost every Japanese has learned something about Anne Frank through the diary, manga comic book adaptations, or anime films. And as French journalist Alain Lewkovitz explains, "the Anne Frank-Japan connection is based on a kinship of victims ... [But t]hey don't think of the countless Anne Franks their troops created in Korea and China..."[46]

---

[41] See Kenzaburo Oe, "Preface to the English edition," in *Hiroshima Notes*, trans. D. L. Swain and T. Yonezawa (New York: Marion Boyars, 1995), 9. The Japanese original was written in 1963.

[42] John Dower, "The Bombed: Hiroshima and Nagasaki in Japanese Memory," *Diplomatic History* 19, no. 2 (1995): 275–95 (here 281).

[43] Robert Jay Lifton, *Death in Life. Survivors of Hiroshima* (Chapel Hill: University of North Carolina Press, 1991), 322.

[44] James J. Orr, *The Victim as Hero: Ideologies of Peace and National Identity in Postwar Japan* (Honolulu: University of Hawaii Press, 2001), 52.

[45] Lisa Yoneyama, *Hiroshima Traces: Time, Space, and the Dialectics of Memory* (Berkeley: University of California Press, 1999), 25.

[46] Quoted in Jewish Telegraphic Agency, "Why Are the Japanese So Fascinated With Anne Frank?" *Haaretz*, January 22, 2014, https://www.haaretz.com/jewish/anne-frank-the-japanese-anime-1.5314070.

The Japanese career of Saint Maksymilian Kolbe is less well known than the Anne Frank syndrome, and it is much more complicated. Canonized in 1982 as a martyr for agreeing to be killed in Auschwitz in place of a fellow-inmate, Father Kolbe had spent time in Nagasaki as a missionary between 1930 and 1936. During those years, Nagai Takashi, the funeral orator of 1945 and himself known as the saint of Nagasaki, had visited Father Kolbe in the Hongochi monastery in Nagasaki and recorded his admiration for the priest. As the historical centre of Japanese Catholicism, Nagasaki was the focus of memory of the past persecution of Catholics in Japan. Kolbe's career at key sites of national and Catholic martyrdom promoted a very particular mnemonic nexus of Polish and Japanese (Catholic) victimhood. The moves for his beatification in 1971 and canonization in 1982 involved efforts to strengthen that nexus.[47]

Endō Shūsaku, a famous Catholic liberal novelist, published the serial novel *Onna no isshō* in the popular progressive daily newspaper *Asahi Shimbun* in 1980–1982.[48] The novel intertwines the love story between two young Christians in wartime Nagasaki with Father Kolbe's martyrdom at Auschwitz. The resulting impression is that the deaths of both Nagasaki and Auschwitz victims were the work of Providence, a redemptive self-sacrifice for the sake of the peaceful future of humankind. Endō Shūsaku's short essay depicting Father Kolbe's death in Auschwitz featured in high school literature textbooks and is and still widely read among Japanese teenagers. In his interpretation, the highest love is to sacrifice one's own life to save that of another—an act of altruism that deserves the name miracle (*kiseki*).[49]

It is intriguing to note that Sono Ayako, one of Japanese Prime Minister Abe's informal advisers, provoked an online storm by writing that South Africa's apartheid policies had been good for Whites, Asians, and Africans. She has praised apartheid as a model of how Japan could expand

---

[47] See Jie-Hyun, Lim, "Kimyōna Hēchi—Makisimiriano Korubeto Nagasaki Hibakushano Shinsēka (A Strange Juxtaposition-Maximilian Kolbe and the Sacralization of the Nagasaki A-Bomb Victims)," in *Sengo Nihon Bunka Saikō*, ed. Tsuboi Hideto (Tōkyō: Sanninsha, 2019), 74–103.

[48] English edition: Endō Shūsaku, *Sachiko*, trans. Van C. Gessell (New York: Columbia University Press, 2020).

[49] Endō Shūsaku, "Korube Shinpu," *Shinpenkokugosōgō Kaiteban* (Tōkyo: Taishukanshoten, 2018), 186.

immigration.⁵⁰ Sono's ultra-nationalist and racist public remarks are well known, but the fact that she has been an admirer of Father Kolbe is not. Two years after his beatification, she published the novel *Kiseki* (miracles), which includes a documentary biography and a fictional narrative in which the protagonist travels in search of the sites and the truth of Kolbe's miracles. Sono's interpretation of "miracle" shares with that of the liberal Endō Shūsaku its emphasis on the highest love to sacrifice one's own life to save another, though she is more fascinated with the patriotic myth of Father Kolbe and his family.⁵¹

It is not particularly surprising that the story of a Polish Catholic martyr became entangled with the history of the suffering of Japanese Catholics in Nagasaki. Kolbe's missionary life really was entwined with the lives of the Catholic *hibakusha* there. But a key element of his story is missing from the Japanese reception. The agents of Japanese memory have maintained total silence on the question of Kolbe's antisemitism, and this is true even among progressive Catholic intellectuals in Japan. When his beatification was announced in 1971, Jan Józef Lipski pointed out the antisemitic tendencies of Kolbe's journal *Mały Dziennik*.⁵² And public discussion of Kolbe's antisemitism was not confined to Poland; his canonization in 1982 reignited the controversy, which the *New York Times* and *Washington Post* widely covered.⁵³ The silence of Japanese Catholics on Kolbe's antisemitism cannot be easily explained. Finding an explanation would help us to assess Japanese memory culture in the postwar period.

---

⁵⁰ Elaine Lies and Takashi Umekawa, "Japan PM ex-adviser praises apartheid in embarrassment for Abe," *Reuters*, February 13, 2015, https://www.reuters.com/article/japan-apartheid/japan-pm-ex-adviser-praises-apartheid-in-embarrassment-for-abe-idUSL4N0VN1PV20150213.

⁵¹ Sono Ayako, *Miracles: A Novel*, trans. Kevin Doak (Portland, ME: Merwin Asia, 2016), 15, 63, 68, 101–2. See also Phillip Gabriel, *Spirit Matters: The Transcendent in Modern Japanese Literature* (Honolulu: University of Hawaii Press, 2006).

⁵² Jan Józef Lipski, "Ojciec Kolbe i *Mały Dziennik*," *Tygodnik Powszechny*, Nr. 38 (1182), 19. IX. 1971.

⁵³ Richard Cohen, "Sainthood," *Washington Post*, December 14, 1982; Binder, "Franciszek Gajowniczek Dead; Priest Died for Him at Auschwitz," *New York Times*, March 15, 1995; John Gross, "Life Saving," *The New York Review of Books*, February 17, 1983; Daniel Schlafly, Warren Green and John Gross, "Kolbe and Anti-Semitism," *The New York Review of Books*, April 14, 1983.

Comfort Women, American-Armenians, and Performative Nationalism

A monument to the Korean comfort women was unveiled in front of the Bergen County courthouse in New Jersey on March 8, International Women's Day, in 2013. Alongside monuments commemorating American slavery, the Holocaust, the Armenian genocide, and the Irish potato famine, a new memorial stone to Korean comfort women took its place in the county's "ring of honor," part of a memory island outside the courthouse. The event exemplified the transpacific migration of the memory of the Korean comfort women. The institutional collaboration between the Korean American Civic Empowerment (KACE) organization and the Kupferberg Holocaust Center accelerated that transpacific memory campaign. The two jointly organized a meeting of Korean comfort women and Jewish American Holocaust survivors in the auditorium of Queensborough Community College on December 13, 2011—a striking example of the global entanglement of migrated memories. The meeting received broad media coverage in Korea.[54]

The mnemonic confluence of the Holocaust and comfort women in New York City epitomizes the extraterritoriality of a global memory of World War II. However, Japanese deniers of the comfort women history and nationalist memory activists began to mobilize in the transpacific memory space too. They appealed to the White House, Congress, and local governments to remove the comfort women monuments by arguing that comfort women were volunteer prostitutes and complaining that Korean nationalists were lying in order to dishonor the Japanese nation. The USA thus became a battlefield as the East Asian memory wars overflowed into the transpacific memory space. The damage done to the regional anti-communist alliance by the memory competition around forced labor and the comfort women is indicated by 2019's accelerating crisis in relations among the parties to the GSOMIA (General Security of

---

[54] No Ch'anghyon, "mi chŏngbu 1ho wianbugirimbi nyujŏjisŏ chemakshik," *Newsis*, March 9, 2013, https://newsis.com/view/?id=NISX20130309_0011904596; Korean American Civic Empowerment, "Compilation of News Articles on Comfort Women Survivors and Holocaust Survivors' Meeting," December 21, 2011, accessed March 8, 2020, http://us.kace.org/2011/compilation-of-news-articles-on-comfort-women-survivors-and-holocaust-survivors%27-meeting/.

Military Information Agreement)—South Korea, Japan, and the USA.[55] Following Bergen County, the City Council of Glendale, California, approved plans for a monument to the Korean comfort women by a vote of four to one on July 9, 2013. Despite the lobbying of Japanese nationalists, Glendale City Council was determined on the comfort women issue. There are two Armenian names, Ara Najarian and Zareh Sinanyan, among those of council members who voted for the plan.[56] Given that Armenian Americans make up about 40% of the city's 200,000 inhabitants, making it the second biggest Armenian settlement in the world after Yerevan, the presence of two of them on the council is not surprising.[57] What is intriguing is the address made by Armenian-American Council members at the unveiling of the comfort women statue.

Ara Najarian called the unveiling "a moment of pride for the City of Glendale" and expressed his hope that the monument could be "a part of the healing process" for the surviving comfort women. Zareh Sinanyan, the first Armenian-born politician to sit on the Glendale City Council and the grandson of an Armenian genocide survivor, also spoke, emphasising how his own memory of the Armenian genocide and its denial by the Turkish state had made him sensitive to the comfort women issue. Presumably, the political calculation of appealing to Glendale's 20,000 Korean-American residents also informed his speech.

Still more impressive for its display of cosmopolitan memory is the ReflectSpace Gallery in Glendale City Library. Designed to explore and reflect on major human atrocities, ReflectSpace provides a range of exhibits on memories.[58] The inaugural exhibition, "Landscape of Memory: Witnesses and Remnants of Genocide," in May–June 2017 reflected on the Armenian Genocide through the cross-disciplinary work of witnesses, survivors, and artists. The second exhibition, "Do the Right Thing," which focused on the comfort women, was presented between July 20 and September 3, 2017. Armenian Americans Ara and Anahid Oshagan and

[55] Choe Sang-Hun, "South Korea Resists U.S. Pressure to Improve Ties With Japan," *New York Times*, November 15, 2019, https://www.nytimes.com/2019/11/15/world/asia/south-korea-japan-intelligence-sharing.html.

[56] Rafu Staff, "Glendale Approves Comfort Women Memorial," *Rafu Shinpo*, July 15, 2013, http://www.rafu.com/2013/07/glendale-approves-comfort-women-memorial/.

[57] Chris McCormick, "Armenian Exceptionalism," *The Atlantic*, April 4, 2016, https://www.theatlantic.com/business/archive/2016/04/glendale-armenians/475926/.

[58] "ReflectSpace," City of Glendale, accessed March 17, 2020, https://www.glendaleca.gov/government/departments/library-arts-culture/reflectspace.

Korean American Monica Hye Yeon Jun co-curated works by twelve international documentarians and artists. The exhibition's key theme was the "tension between the inability to speak about personal trauma and the deep human urge to tell" characteristic of many survivor experiences.[59] Subsequent exhibitions "Wake: The Afterlife of Slavery," "i am: Narratives of the Holocaust," "in/visible—Negotiating the US-Mexico Border," and "Nonlinear Histories—Transnational Memory of Trauma" show explicitly how dedicated the gallery is to mapping the global memory space.

It is heartening to note that in stark contrast to the position taken by Japanese-American right-wing nationalists *Rafu Shimpo*, the Japanese-American community newspaper in Little Tokyo in Los Angeles, published a very sympathetic report on the unveiling ceremony. The NCRR (Nikkei for Civil Rights & Redress) has also been supportive of commemorating comfort women in the USA. The NCRR was founded in 1980 to call for compensation and redress for 120,000 Japanese Americans interned during World War II. It helped many internees to speak out at the 1981 hearings of the Commission on Wartime Relocation and Internment of Civilians. At the same time, it actively supported memory activism around the comfort women as part of a wider commitment to emancipatory memory politics and fighting discrimination. After September 11, 2001, the NCRR established a 9/11 Committee to collaborate with the Muslim Public Affairs Council, the Council on American-Islamic Relations, and the American Arab Anti-Discrimination Committee.[60]

The unanticipated collaboration of the Armenian-American community and Japanese Americans of the NCRR in commemorating Korean comfort women in Glendale is an example of vernacular cosmopolitan memory in which mnemonic solidarity almost seems to have been realized. A closer look, however, reveals a more complex picture. Zareh Sinanyan had to apologize for posting racist, homophobic, and vulgar comments on YouTube, "many of which appeared centered around Armenia's geopolitical enemies"[61]—actions in stark contrast with the soli-

---

[59] Chuck Wike, "New Exhibition at Downtown Glendale Central Library: Do the Right Thing—(dis)comfort women," City of Glendale, accessed March 17, 2020, https://www.glendaleca.gov/Home/Components/News/News/5389/1097?arch=1&npage=12.

[60] "About NCRR," NCRR—Nikkei for Civil Rights and Redress, accessed March 8, 2020, http://www.ncrr-la.org/about.html.

[61] Brittany Levine, "Glendale Councilman Zareh Sinanyan apologizes for racist postings," *Los Angeles Times*, May 1, 2013.

dary sentiments of his Glendale speech. Moreover, in a private talk with Korean-American memory activists, Sinanyan disagreed with the comparison they made between the Armenian genocide and the Japanese military sexual slavery.[62] His remarks implied that only the Holocaust is actually comparable to the "Armenocide," which should not be placed on a par with the petty tragedy of the comfort women. Mnemonic solidarity remains subject to the agony of competition.

To be sure, the globalization of the comfort women issue would hardly have been possible without mnemonic solidarity. Until the early 1990s, comfort women were silenced and erased from the national and regional memory in East Asia.[63] Even when the suppressed memory surfaced in Korea in 1991, it remained a matter of "nationalized sexuality": When memory activists proposed building a monument at Independence Hall of Korea, they were turned down on the pretext that there was not enough space in the most spacious memorial site in Korea. Comfort women did not fit the Hall's heroic narrative. Postcolonial Korea's dominant patriarchal memory thus marginalized and suppressed a key dimension of the country's wartime suffering.[64]

It was the heightened sensitivity to sexual violence provoked by the civil war in former Yugoslavia and the Rwandan genocide that moved the comfort women into the global mnemospace. A reflection on the sexual abuse in former Yugoslavia sharpened the awareness of women's rights as an inalienable, integral, and indivisible part of human rights. The International Criminal Tribunals for the former Yugoslavia and Rwanda (ICTY and ICTR) included rape as a crime against humanity, providing a language for the Women's International War Crimes Tribunal on Japan's Military Sexual Slavery that convened in Tokyo in 2000.[65] The composition of the Tokyo tribunal itself demonstrates the significance of the global memory space. Gabrielle Kirk McDonald, the former president of the ICTY, and Patricia Viseur-Sellers, Legal Advisor on Gender Related Crimes to both the ICTY and ICTR, acted as judges and chief prosecutors. Eight regional

[62] General Secretary of KACE, in discussion with the author, KACE Office, New York City, July 4, 2014.
[63] See Carol Gluck's chapter in this volume.
[64] Hyunah Yang, "Hankookin gunwuianburŭl giŏkhandanŭngeot (Remembering Korean comfort women)," in *Wihŏmhan Yŏsŏng [Dangerous Women]*, eds. Elaine H. Kim and Chungmoo Choi, trans. Eunmi Park, (Seoul: Samin, 2002), 157–76 (here 175).
[65] Maki Kimura, *Unfolding the "Comfort Women" Debates: Modernity, Violence, Women's Voices* (Basingstoke: Palgrave Macmillan, 2016), 6–8.

teams of prosecutors, including a joint team from South and North Korea, presented cases on behalf of the former comfort women.[66]

The judgment of the Tokyo Tribunal did not carry legally binding force. But its conviction of the Japanese state and the dead emperor Hirohito for "war crimes and crimes against humanity" had symbolic significance. The final judgment reads: "The crimes committed against the survivors remain one of the great unremedied injustices of the Second World War. There are no museums, no graves for the unknown comfort woman, no education of future generations, and no judgment days, for the victims of Japan's military sexual slavery. Many of the women who have come forward to fight for justice have died unsung heroes."[67] As Carol Gluck argues in this volume "Just as the Holocaust became a global example of genocide, so did the comfort women become a touchstone for new international law relating to the violence against women in war."

If Korean nationalism initially operated to suppress the memory of the comfort women, this opening up of a global conversation about them has also drawn nationalist memory activists into the commemoration business. The aborted plan to install a comfort women statue in the German city of Freiburg offers another insight the multiple political uses of a memory icon and also into the ways in which mnemonic solidarity can be buffeted by the cross-currents of global-transnational and local memory politics. In September 2016 Tae-young Yeom, the mayor of the South Korean city of Suwon, proposed to send a comfort woman statue to Suwon's partner city Freiburg. Initially, Freiburg's mayor Dieter Salomon welcomed it as the kind of gift that is usual between sister cities. As a committed Green Party politician, Salomon was also memory-conscious, an advocate of critical engagement with Germany's Nazi past. But he had to withdraw his decision, partly because of local voices arguing that it would be a scandal to build a comfort woman statue when there was not yet any memorial to the victims of German wartime sexual slavery and violence. The angry reaction from citizens of Matsuyama, Freiburg's partner city in Japan, also inclined Mayor Salomon to rethink his original move.[68]

---

[66] Rumi Sakamoto, "The Women's International War Crimes Tribunal on Japan's Military Sexual Slavery: A Legal and Feminist Approach to the 'Comfort Women' Issue," *New Zealand Journal of Asian Studies* 3 (2001): 49–58 (here 49–50).

[67] Judges of the Women's International War Crimes Tribunal on Japan's Military Sexual Slavery, "Transcript of Oral Judgment," December 4, 2001, accessed March 8, 2020, http://iccwomen.org/wigjdraft1/Archives/oldWCGJ/tokyo/summary.html.

[68] Esther Felden, "Freiburg und die Trostfrau," *Deutsche Welle*, September 21, 2016, http://www.dw.com/de/freiburg-und-die-trostfrau/a-19563885.

The story does not end here. In November 2016, The Korean Council for the Women Drafted for Military Sexual Slavery by Japan, a nationalist feminist NGO, made Mayor Yeom the first to win the Council's special prize designed for local policymakers who promote and globalize the comfort women issue.[69] On International Women's Day in 2017, thanks to Mayor Yeom's tireless efforts, a replica of the comfort woman statue that stands in front of the Japanese embassy in Seoul was unveiled in the Nepal-Himalaya-Pavillon in Wiesent, a Bavarian village with a population of under 2500.[70] Neither German nor Korean media reports explain why the Nepal-Himalaya-Pavillon in Wiesent was chosen for this gesture.

This event was performed entirely out of context, out of history, and out of memory. Perhaps it was not the German residents of Wiesent, but the Korean voters at home that the comfort women statue was designed to address. Around the same time, the provincial assembly of Gyunggi-do province, to which Suwon belongs, resolved to erect a comfort woman statue on Dokdo/Takeshima—a cluster of rocks in the Sea of Japan which is the subject of an angry territorial dispute between Korea and Japan. As the chairperson of Gyunggi-do provincial assembly stressed the principle of "human rights" in this resolution,[71] he revealed the open secret of how mnemonic nationalism appropriates and vulgarizes cosmopolitan memory. The global memory space provided Korea's Quixotic nationalists with a brand new playground, and local politicians were able to exploit Korean victimhood nationalism, which is deeply rooted at the local government level, to raise their national and even global profiles. Memory activism around the comfort women still threatens to reinforce a victimhood nationalism that has become more performative, visualized, intimate, and entrenched in the everyday life of postcolonial Korea.

---

[69] Yi Minu, "yŏmt'aeyŏng suwŏnshijang, chŏngdaehyŏp t'rt'ŭkpyŏlsangt' susang," *Newspeak*, November 21, 2016, http://www.newspeak.kr/news/articleView.html?idxno=116422.

[70] Stefan Gruber, "'Trostfrau' mahnt zum Frieden," *Mittelbayeriscshe Zeitung*, March 12, 2017, https://www.mittelbayerische.de/region/regensburg-land/gemeinden/wiesent/trostfrau-mahnt-zum-frieden-21411-art1496089.html. My thanks to Tanja Vaitulevich for the information of this bizarre event.

[71] Hong Yong Duck, "kyŏnggidoŭihoe orhae ane toktoe p'yŏnghwaŭi sonyŏsang seugiro," *Hankyoreh*, January 16, 2017, http://www.hani.co.kr/arti/society/area/778893.html.

Critical Relativization in Postcolonial Perspective

The mnemonic confluence of the Holocaust, colonialist crimes, and Stalinist terror characterizes global memory formation in the post-Cold War era, an era in which "multidirectional memory" is not yet free from hegemonic memory politics.[72] A reflection on the ways in which memories of Holocaust and Gulag, of Auschwitz and Nagasaki, of the Armenian genocide and the comfort women, of Mississippi, Robben Island and the *Generalgouvernement*, have been and might be globally connected reveals a tension inherent in the global memory formation itself. Whether at the official or the vernacular level, remembrance is permanently pulled between forces of de-territorialization and re-territorialization. The simple generic juxtaposition of three traumas (or victimhoods)—or any two of them—does not necessarily produce a rosy cosmopolitan memory. National memories have competed for the status of hegemon in global memory formation, and the result has been the hierarchization of victimhood. In post-communist Eastern Europe and the postcolonial tricontinent, what promised to be a cosmopolitan memory of Holocaust has been appropriated to serve mnemonic nationalism. In places where victims and victimizers cohabit, an indigenized Holocaust remembrance has worked as a screen memory to veil the dark history of the victims' own crimes.

Cosmopolitan memory is thus not free from nationalist appropriation. Indeed, against our expectations, it provides mnemonic nationalism with persistent moral leverage, thus intensifying the struggle for mnemonic hegemony among conflicting national memories. Holocaust memory as it circulates globally is particularly vulnerable to nationalist appropriation, perhaps because it occupies a position of absolute morality.[73] And the unique success of Holocaust survivors in claiming material restitution makes their moral claim, in all its absoluteness, an object of emulation for other traumatized groups. It is a paradox but no surprise

---

[72] See Rothberg, *Multidirectional Memory*.

[73] The verdict of the European Court of Justice on December 17, 2017 that denying the Armenian genocide belongs to the domain of the freedom of speech, while the denial of the Holocaust is a crime transcending the freedom of speech, is a case in point. See Ofer Aderet and Reuters, "European Court: Denying Armenian 'Genocide' Is No Crime: Judges draw distinction between Armenian case and the Holocaust of the Jews," *Haaretz*, December 18, 2013, https://www.haaretz.com/european-court-no-crime-to-deny-armenian-genocide-1.5301268.

that the Holocaust as an object of cosmopolitan memory is frequently abused to justify nationalist remembrance in Eastern Europe and East Asia in the post-Cold War era. This is not because the Holocaust has "no real resonance" outside of Europe, Israel, and the USA.[74] Israel, the USA, and Western Europe were never reluctant to politicize, instrumentalize, and abuse Holocaust memory. If anything, the presence of real survivors in the "Western" countries made it easier to authenticate, justify, and facilitate the politicization of the Holocaust memory. In short, the cosmopolitanization of the Holocaust has intensified mnemonic nationalism as much as it has contributed to mnemonic solidarity in the global memory formation.

Zygmunt Bauman's warning that the Holocaust is a logical outcome not of premodern barbarity, but of Western modernity gives us a clue to how to connect postcolonial criticism to global memory formation in the post-Cold War era. His postmodernist critique of the Holocaust disquiets "the moral comfort of self-exculpation" by the non-German West by shattering the complacent binary of mad perpetrators and innocent victims. If it is a "legitimate outcome of the civilizing process" in modern society, the Holocaust becomes "our" problem beyond the German-Jewish encounter.[75] In the same way, a postcolonial critique can alert us to the mnemonic nationalism inherent in triple victimhood claims. Attentiveness to the ways in which anti-colonial nationalism operates not as an alternative but as an accomplice to colonialism exposes the ambivalence of colonialist desire and frustration among the colonized. It can help us to rescue the memory of colonial victimhood in the tri-continent from mnemonic nationalism. And the critical gaze of postcolonialism can be extended to Eastern Europe, where the analogy between the Slavic East under the Nazi occupation of the "Third Europe," the socialist colonies under the Stalinist red empire, and the postcolonial states of the "Third World" was familiar. The postcolonial entanglement of triple victimhood is one of keys to understanding the global memory formation in the post-Cold War era.

By way of conclusion, I propose critical relativization and radical juxtaposition as antidotes to the nationalist appropriation of cosmopolitan memory. This is different from what came to be known as the relativization of the Holocaust in the course of the German *Historikerstreit* of the

---

[74] Alon Confino, "The Holocaust as a Symbolic Manual: The French Revolution, the Holocaust, and Global Memories," in *Marking Evil: Holocaust Memory in the Global Age* eds. Amos Goldberg and Haim Hazan (New York: Berghahn Books, 2015), 56–70 (here 56).

[75] Bauman, *Modernity and the Holocaust*, xii, 28.

late 1980s, when Ernst Nolte and other right-wing historians proposed to "explain"—and in effect justify—the crimes of National Socialism by presenting Nazism as a response to Bolshevik terror.[76] This episode developed into a debate about West German national identity which was substantially overtaken by the end of the Cold War. It briefly tarnished comparative approaches and challenges to the historical uniqueness of the Holocaust with the suspicion of apologetic nationalism. But comparison remains a critical methodology in historical studies, and in any case, as Charles Maier argued then, "comparability cannot really exculpate."[77]

What matters is not generic relativization or comparability but the "political relativization of responsibility."[78] For example, the focus on the human actors and questions of responsibility allows us to interrogate assertions of the historical uniqueness or ineffability of the Holocaust, and more particularly those that subsume the complex Holocaust events into the mass murder of a single people, the Shoah. As Geoff Eley pointed out at the time of the *Historikerstreit*, the exclusive focus on Shoah "tends to free other, less universally abhorred aspects of Nazism (like the crimes against labor), let alone other parts of the killing program (like the murder of gypsies, Poles, Soviet P.O.W.s, homosexuals, and so on) from attention."[79] We need to see even the mass murder of the Jews in the context of processes and practices that are open to *both* historical explanation *and* ethical and forensic judgment.

Arguably, the memory wars in post-communist Eastern Europe and postcolonial tri-continent represent a second, global wave of the *Historikerstreit*. Memories and narratives of the past are now more diverse, contradictory, localized, and multiple than they were when subject to ideological division on the single axis of the Cold War. The cosmopolitanization of Holocaust memory remains an undeniable phenomenon in the post-Cold War era. But the global memory formation involves more than the mere transposition of Holocaust memory onto colonial genocide and Stalinist terror. Neither, from the viewpoint of global memory formation,

---

[76] See Siobahn Kattago, *Ambiguous Memory: The Nazi Past and German National Identity* (Westport, CT: Praeger, 2001), 56–62; Geoff Eley, "Nazism, Politics and the Image of the Past: Thoughts on the West German Historikerstreit 1986–1987," *Past & Present*, no. 121 (1988): 171–208 (here 173).

[77] Charles S. Maier, *The Unmasterable Past: History, Holocaust and German National Identity* (Cambridge, MA: Harvard University Press, 1997), 1.

[78] Ibid., xii.

[79] Eley, "Nazism, Politics and the Image of the Past," 174.

are we required to make an either/or choice between uniqueness and relativization. What I call critical relativization should make it possible for us to consider other victims empathetically, and to resist the temptation of prioritizing our own victimhood. Similarly, the critical juxtaposition of different memories that avoids the compulsion to make systematic or causal connections can help us to perform non-hierarchical acts of comparison in the global memory space.[80]

---

[80] On critical juxtaposition, see Susan Stanford Friedman, "Planetarity: Musing Modernist Studies," *Modernism/Modernity* 17, no. 3 (2010): 471–99 (here 493–94).

Open Access This chapter is licensed under the terms of the Creative Commons Attribution 4.0 International License (http://creativecommons.org/licenses/by/4.0/), which permits use, sharing, adaptation, distribution and reproduction in any medium or format, as long as you give appropriate credit to the original author(s) and the source, provide a link to the Creative Commons licence and indicate if changes were made.

The images or other third party material in this chapter are included in the chapter's Creative Commons licence, unless indicated otherwise in a credit line to the material. If material is not included in the chapter's Creative Commons licence and your intended use is not permitted by statutory regulation or exceeds the permitted use, you will need to obtain permission directly from the copyright holder.

CHAPTER 3

Europe's Melancholias: Diasporas in Contention and the Unravelings of the Postwar Settlement

Eve Rosenhaft

Fig. 3.1 Still from the film *Where Hands Touch* (Tantrum Films)

E. Rosenhaft (✉)
School of Histories, Languages & Cultures, University of Liverpool, Liverpool, UK
e-mail: dan85@liverpool.ac.uk

© The Author(s) 2021
J.-H. Lim, E. Rosenhaft (eds.), *Mnemonic Solidarity*, Entangled Memories in the Global South,
https://doi.org/10.1007/978-3-030-57669-1_3

Abstract Rosenhaft explores some ways in which discourses of human rights, racism and antisemitism that emerged in the global North after 1945 have been appropriated, complicated and disrupted in this century's memory conflicts. She examines Black Holocaust fictions in the light of changes in the global Black diaspora, and reflects on the recent debates on antisemitism and Holocaust memory that place diasporic actors in contention as well as on the populist trope of a "white, Christian Europe". Following Paul Gilroy's use of the term "postcolonial melancholia" to characterize British nostalgia for empire, she identifies analogous forms of nostalgia driving the current memory wars, and deploys the notions of "post-Holocaust" and "post-imperial" melancholias as complementary responses to the challenges posed by the (re-)emergence of a multicultural Europe.

Keywords Holocaust memory • Black diaspora • Antisemitism • Israel • Melancholia • Multidirectional memory

This chapter reflects on the ways in which, in the twenty-first century, generational change and shifting patterns of migration and diaspora have combined to complicate and challenge the discourses of human rights, racism and antisemitism that emerged in Europe and the United States in the wake of the Second World War and the Holocaust. These discourses underpinned a structure of what Michael Rothberg called "multidirectional memory" which, fragile though it has always been, seemed for a time to promise a degree of solidarity among the victims of genocide, war and colonialism living in the global North or raised in its philosophical traditions, and reflected the hegemonic power of a vision of "human rights" allied to a politics of redress for historical wrongs.[1] The twenty-first century has witnessed a falling-out among the parties to that solidarity and a renewal of memory contests, even in the liberal West. These are manifested equally in publicly debated anxieties about antisemitism that center for the first time on parties of the left, in the historical (including Holocaust) revisionism of populist and right-wing movements and governments, and in the renewal of claims of national sovereignty in opposition to human rights discourse.

---

[1] Michael Rothberg, *Multidirectional Memory: Remembering the Holocaust in the Age of Decolonization* (Stanford: Stanford University Press, 2009).

In the European frame, an important source of antagonism is the failure of white Europe as a whole to come to terms with the legacies of colonialism—including the demographic consequences of two world wars. In the British case, Paul Gilroy has characterized the pathology of this failure in terms of "postcolonial melancholia"—a nostalgia for empire that refuses to accept its lived and living consequences in the here and now.[2] I want to suggest that it is possible to identify analogous forms of nostalgia driving the current memory wars, as forms of metropolitan amnesia about the character of imperial polities that manifest as melancholia come up against new claims of *physical* presence (diaspora) that are still realizing the implications of empire in the metropolis. This is true not only of the historical colonial metropoles of Western Europe, but also of the former continental empires of Eastern and Central Europe, *and* those parts of the global North that partake of the mnemospace created by the post-1945 settlement and re-molded by its collapse at the end of the 1980s—the United States and Israel. I tentatively introduce the notions of "post-Holocaust" and "post-imperial" melancholia as complementary responses to the real challenges posed by the (re-)emergence of a multicultural Europe. The first result of this encounter between contending claims on the past has been rage; the question is whether it is possible to go beyond that to new forms of shared ownership of the past.

A feature of these recent developments is the mobilization of diasporic populations both in solidarity with human rights struggles abroad and in defense of "homeland" states *against* human rights claims. The fact of such mobilization is not new; the modern history of migration has seen many episodes in which conflicts in the homeland and the political dispositions they generate have been transposed to the new lands of settlement. And they are a reminder, among other things, of the ambivalence of the dynamic relationship between vernacular and official memory discussed in the introduction to this volume. The modes of mobilization and their consequences shift over time as the who, why and where of migration flows change along with the self-perceptions of homelands.[3] The reconfiguration of diasporas leads to new kinds of conversations within and between them, all of which have a mnemonic dimension. Memory, after all, does not exist without rememberers, and memory communities are

---

[2] Paul Gilroy, *Postcolonial Melancholia* (New York: Columbia University Press, 2005).
[3] Cf Latha Varadarajan, *The Domestic Abroad. Diasporas in International Relations* (Oxford: Oxford University Press, 2010) and the literature cited there.

subject to generational and demographic change. This unpicking of the materiality of cultural memory is key to understanding the prospects for mnemonic solidarity.

Black Holocaust Fictions and Conversations in the Diaspora

I start by considering how the dynamics of *internal* contention within an evolving global diaspora are at work on the familiar territory of "multidirectional memory," namely in the imaginative engagement of contemporary Black cultural producers with the Holocaust. In his chapter in this volume, Jie-Hyun Lim sketches out a still-remembered history of shared human rights struggles between Jewish radicals and Black activists in Europe, America and Europe's settler colonies. To some extent what I call Black Holocaust fiction continues in dialogue with that history. That dialogue has taken on new dimensions in the twenty-first century, and those are the focus of the second section of this chapter. What I explore here is the consequences of the way in which the Afro-diasporic memory space is being reconfigured through the growth of an African and Afro-Caribbean immigrant population in the United States and the emergence of new "Afropean" voices.[4] Those voices challenge the primacy of the transatlantic slavery narrative and its heirs in the United States.

Novels and films produced since 1999 and more particularly since the mid-2000s partake of a moment of intensification of representation of a Black Holocaust experience. This began with the increased circulation of knowledge and information about the experiences of Black people in Nazi Germany and occupied Europe, and it is notable that the three novels that interest me here, *Clifford's Blues* (1999) by John A. Williams, *Half-Blood Blues* (2011) by Esi Edugyan, and *The Book of Harlan* (2016) by Bernice McFadden, all include bibliographies.[5] The bibliographies claim historical authenticity for their stories; they also indicate that the writers are drawing on knowledge of the persecution that was certainly intimated in the 1940s but was then largely forgotten for fifty years. In the English-speaking

---

[4] For a recent work that engages this term critically but affirmatively, see Johny Pitts, *Afropean. Notes from Black Europe* (Harmondsworth: Penguin, 2019).

[5] John A. Williams, *Clifford's Blues* (Minneapolis: Coffee House Press, 1999); Esi Edugyan, *Half-Blood Blues* (London: Serpent's Tail, 2011); Bernice L. McFadden, *The Book of Harlan* (New York: Akashic Books, 2016).

world, television and the internet contributed to the dissemination and popularization of information about Black Holocaust experiences. John Williams was inspired by seeing a photograph of a Black inmate on a visit to Dachau, but Esi Edugyan was one of a younger generation who found the images that piqued their curiosity in books and on the internet.[6] The first English-language television documentary on the subject, *Hitler's Forgotten Victims*, was made for the British broadcaster Channel 4 in 1997 (written by Cameroonian Moise Shewa and directed by Briton David Okuefuna). The year 2002 saw the publication of Clarence Lusane's *Hitler's Black Victims*, the first serious attempt to bring together the published evidence on the subject, and Tina Campt's *Other Germans*, a groundbreaking and theoretically sophisticated work on race and gender in the lives of Afro-Germans persecuted by the Nazis, came out in 2004. In 2006, Raffael Scheck published his study of the German army massacres of French colonial troops in 1940—numerically the largest group of Hitler's Black victims.[7]

New fictions were thus a natural response to the rhythms of public knowledge and interest, as more became knowable about the situation of Black people under Nazism. But they can also be read as reflections the contemporary Black experience. Each of the novelists chooses an African-American man as protagonist, and each of the protagonists either finds himself in a concentration camp or narrowly escapes it after having arrived in Europe as a jazz performer. In a 2011 reflection on the memory contests triggered by the conflict in Palestine, Michael Rothberg implicitly distinguishes between memories as such and the "unavoidable building

---

[6] Gilbert H. Muller, Michael Blaine and Raymond C. Bowen, "Clifford's Blues: A Conversation with John A. Williams," in *Conversations with John A. Williams*, ed. Jeffrey A. Tucker (Jackson, MS: University Press of Mississippi, 2018), 217–26; Maaza Mengiste, "The Place in Between: An Interview with Esi Edugyan," *Callaloo* 36, no. 1 (Winter 2013): 46–51; Esi Edugyan, *Dreaming of Elsewhere. Observations on Home* (Edmonton: University of Alberta Press, 2014); Cath Clarke, "A secret romance: the director who is confronting Nazis, race and bigotry" (Interview with Amma Asante), *The Guardian*, May 3, 2019, https://www.theguardian.com/film/2019/may/03/secret-romance-amma-asante-director-nazis-race-bigotry.

[7] Clarence Lusane, *Hitler's Black Victims. The Historical Experiences of Afro-Germans, European Blacks, Africans, and African Americans in the Nazi Era* (New York: Routledge, 2002); Tina Campt, *Other Germans: Black Germans and the Politics of Race, Gender, and Memory in the Third Reich* (Ann Arbor: Michigan University Press, 2004); Raffael Scheck, *Hitler's African Victims. The German Massacres of Black French Soldiers in 1940* (Cambridge: Cambridge University Press, 2006).

blocks or morphemes *of* memory," adding that the fact that those morphemes are combined in multidirectional ways does not have any particular political valence.[8] When the authors of Black Holocaust fictions place African-American jazzmen in Nazi concentration camps, what they are doing is to mobilize highly recognizable "morphemes" from intersecting memory traditions. The relationship between the narratives thus generated and what is known about the reality of Hitler's Black victims, however, is highly attenuated. Even in proportion to the relatively small Black presence in Germany, there were few Black people in concentration camps. Most victims were settled colonial immigrants or German-born Blacks and they suffered mainly from loss of access to education, training and work, denial of citizenship, forced labor and the threat and reality of compulsory sterilization. While each of the novels acknowledges in some degree the historical reality of Afro-German and other non-American Black victims, the African-American perspective remains central. In *The Book of Harlan*, the depiction of life in Buchenwald is distinguished by its deployment of an extremely sensationalized version of the concentration camp morpheme. But the concentration camp story is simply an episode, though in some senses the climax, in what is essentially a twentieth-century family saga based on the author's own family history.

I want to propose that the timing and shape of these fictions has something to do with the shifting balance between optimism and pessimism in Black memory communities. This seems to me to be particularly true of Williams and McFadden, both African Americans (Edugyan was born in Canada to Ghanaian parents). For their protagonists, Europe's jazz metropolises Berlin and Paris, which historically figured in the African-American imagination as spaces of liberty and escape, become places of incarceration and death. In fact *Clifford's Blues* is modeled on a slave narrative and portrays its protagonist's survival for twelve years in Dachau as a return to slavery, in his case forced domestic service to an SS officer.[9] An earlier working of the motif of return, Octavia E. Butler's 1979 *Kindred*, although not itself a Holocaust fiction, anticipates this. In *Kindred*, a twentieth-century African-American woman who finds herself repeatedly transported back to a slave plantation to ensure the survival of her white

---

[8] Michael Rothberg, "From Gaza to Warsaw: Mapping Multidirectional Memory," *Criticism* 53, no. 4 (2011): 523–48.

[9] Heidi Elisabeth Bollinger, "Crimes of Racial and Generic Mixing in John A. Williams's *Clifford's Blues*," *Journal of Narrative Theory* 44, no. 2 (2014): 267–303.

great-grandfather has recourse to reading about Nazi concentration camps in her effort to understand the psychological regime of the plantation.[10]

The world of these novels is a world of imperiled Black bodies; their vision is a pessimistic one. The publications of the past twenty years reflect not only the availability of new materials for envisioning the Holocaust past but the present of "post-postracial America," of Black Lives Matter, of unsanctioned police killings and, most recently, the tolerated assertiveness of organized white racism in the public sphere.[11] And these grounds for pessimism are not restricted to the United States. The move to the right signaled by Donald Trump's election in the United States was echoed by the outcome of the Brexit referendum in Britain and all that has followed, and indeed by the resurgence of the populist right across Europe. Literary Afro-pessimism and the Black Lives Matter movement have also become part of the German political and cultural scene.[12]

In Britain, Paul Gilroy's 2005 diagnosis of "postcolonial melancholia" mourned the slipping away of "the ludic, cosmopolitan energies and democratic possibilities so evident in the postcolonial metropolis" that he had identified in his earlier work. More than ludic possibilities have been lost in the succeeding decade and a half. In what has become known in the United Kingdom as the Windrush Scandal, between 2012 and 2019 a still unknown number of Black Britons were denied access to housing, jobs and healthcare and 88 were deported to countries in the Caribbean where they had been born but never lived; some died abroad, alone and in fear, while the deaths of others still in the United Kingdom were hastened by the stress of their situation. The victims of what the then Prime Minister celebrated as a "hostile environment" for illegal immigrants had arrived as children or been born in Britain between 1948 and 1973, while their parents, as colonial subjects, still carried British passports under the old imperial dispensation. Their status as British nationals was affirmed in law when immigration rules were tightened in the wake of decolonization in the

---

[10] Octavia E. Butler, *Kindred* (New York: Doubleday, 1979).

[11] For a recent use of "post-postracial," see Alison Landsberg, "Post-postracial America. On *Westworld* and the Smithsonian National Museum of African American History and Culture," *Cultural Politics* 14, no. 2 (July 2018): 198–215.

[12] Priscilla Layne, "The Darkening of Europe: Afrofuturist Ambitions and Afropessimist Fears in Damir Lukacevic's Dystopian Film *Transfer* (2010)," *Seminar* 55, no. 1 (February 2019): 54–75; Kevina King, "Black, People of Color and Migrant Lives Should Matter: Racial Profiling, Police Brutality and Whiteness in Germany," in *Rethinking Black German Studies*, eds. Tiffany N. Florvil and Vanessa D. Plumly (Oxford: Peter Lang, 2018), 169–96.

1970s. But that status was nowhere documented, so when they were challenged to prove that they were not in the country illegally they could not.[13] In effect, the system—the archive and the people whose job it was to manage the archive and the polity itself—had forgotten that they existed.

It is not surprising, then, that Black writers and filmmakers outside the United States are also producing Holocaust fictions.[14] Moreover, they are deploying some of the same morphemes. But they are using them in rather different ways to place Black Europeans in Holocaust history and to reflect on the issues of race and identity particular to them. Anglophone African migrants of the second generation are notable for the interest they have shown in the Black Holocaust. As noted above, the first television documentary was made by a Black Briton. In an early short film, *The Greatest Escape*, Black British filmmaker John Sealey places a Tirailleur Sénégalais—a French colonial soldier—in a German POW camp to develop a surrealist riff on the still resonant statement "There are no Black Germans." The narrative moves from realistic scenes of capture and racial abuse to a comic conclusion in which the protagonist is able to leave the camp simply by putting on the commandant's coat and rebuking the sentries on his way out—certified German by the uniform and accordingly no longer Black. Sealey describes the film as a reflection on his own experience of invisibility, reinforced by observing the non-presence of Black people in Hollywood movies.[15] In Canadian Esi Edugyan's *Half-Blood Blues*, although African-American Sid is the protagonist-narrator, the narrative centers on his fellow bandsman Hiero, a mixed-race German, who is sent to a concentration camp as a result of Sid's actions. The year 2018 saw the release of Amma Asante's feature film *Where Hands Touch*. The film tells the story of Leyna, the daughter of a French colonial soldier and a German mother, who falls

---

[13] Amelia Gentleman, *The Windrush Betrayal: Exposing the Hostile Environment* (London: Guardian Faber, 2019).

[14] A non-European example with a strong European connection is the plan for a film based on the documented experiences of mixed couples in Nazi Germany under development by the Nigerian web entertainment company EbonyLife Films "AVA AND DUANTE," EbonyLife Films, accessed April 25, 2020, https://ebonylifefilms.com/filmsindevelopment/. EbonyLife's founder and CEO is Mosunmola Abudu, born in London to Nigerian parents.

[15] *The Greatest Escape*, dir. John Sealey (GB 2003); John Sealey, "Black and German: Filming Black History and Experience," in *Africa in Europe. Studies in Transnational Practice in the Long Twentieth Century*, eds. Eve Rosenhaft and Robbie Aitken (Liverpool: Liverpool University Press, 2013), 234–47.

in love with the son of an SS-officer while evading sterilization in 1944 Berlin. Asante, raised in London by Ghanaian parents, tells a complex story about her engagement with this history: Although she has made two films which focus on global Black British history and questions of racial allegiance—*Belle* (2014) and *A United Kingdom* (2016)—*Where Hands Touch* was in fact her first project for a historical drama. Even as a schoolgirl she was fascinated by the Holocaust—caught up in that global circulation of threshold knowledge referred to above. But her own experience of living with outspoken racism in South London led her to want to anatomize white racism at the same time as she reflected on her own Black British identity and the meanings of belonging.[16]

What these cultural producers make of the Holocaust story, and the ways in which their fictions have been received, relate to shifts and asynchronies in the shape of the diaspora that is the source and audience for new historical fictions. The entry into the historical conversation of people of color who are not descendants of enslaved Africans is changing the nature of the conversation within the global Black community. If the relationship of Africans and Afropeans to the Holocaust is mediated by their own experiences of colonialism, postcolonial conflicts and migration, the same is equally true of their relationship to the historical traumas of African Americans. The American critic Michelle Wright has drawn attention to the significance of this. In her book *Physics of Blackness* she insists on the limitations of what she calls the Middle Passage Epistemology, which prioritizes transatlantic slavery and its narratives in the articulation of Black diasporic identity. Against this "genealogical," hierarchical and heteronormative understanding of Black identity she argues for one that acknowledges multiple origins and possible forms of affinity.[17] African and Afropean writers, too, have been critical of claims, explicit and implicit, that the only historically relevant Black experience is (a particular version of) the African-American one.[18]

---

[16] Clarke, "A secret romance"; Amma Asante's home page: "AMMA ASANTE," accessed May 5, 2020, www.ammaasante.com.

[17] Michelle M. Wright, *Physics of Blackness. Beyond the Middle Passage Epistemology* (Minneapolis: University of Minnesota Press, 2015).

[18] For example, Paul Tiyambe Zeleza, "Rewriting the African Diaspora: Beyond The Black Atlantic," *African Affairs* 104, no. 414 (January 2005): 35–68; Aretha Phiri, "Expanding black subjectivities in Toni Morrison's Song of Solomon and Chimamanda Ngozi Adichie's Americanah," *Cultural Studies* 31, no. 1 (2017): 121–42.

Conversely, the first reactions to the trailers for *Where Hands Touch* and following its release in North America reflected a significant degree of *non*-recognition on the part of American viewers of the particularities of the Black European experience. Among the critical responses was a combination of disgust and incredulity at the visible pairing of the Afro-German protagonist with a boy who is not only white but wearing a Nazi uniform. Some viewers were irritated by Asante's inversion of the jazz morpheme: Here, it is the son of a white German fan of Billie Holiday who introduces Leyna to the forbidden music.[19] It is important in this context that Sealey, Edugyan and Asante are all explicit about using stories which place their protagonists in conditions of extreme stress to explore questions of identity for Black people living in majority white communities (like Afropeans both before and since the Second World War), and that for Edugyan and Asante the character who articulates this problem is of mixed race: a German with an African father. It is striking, too, that all three end their narratives of radical imperilment on an optimistic note: I have noted the comic dénouement of *The Greatest Escape*; *Half-Blood Blues* ends with a reconciliation between Sid and Hiero, who has survived the camps, while Asante's Leyna survives to give birth to a mixed race child of her own.

For all their optimism these texts—and their authors—offer warnings against racism, but this generation of Afro-diasporic cultural producers has its own questions to ask of history. It is positioning itself somewhere between the undifferentiated "humanity" of global-genocide discourse with its *analogies* between slavery, colonialism and Holocaust and the Black Europeans who were more than accidental victims of Nazi genocide. The more immediate sense that if this is not *my* history, it might have been, reflects not just the emergence of a global memory space but a conviction of global citizenship that goes beyond the diasporic—and which its subjects rightly see as being under threat from the rise of new forms of populism and exclusionism.

---

[19] See Kate Erbland, "'Where Hands Touch' Filmmaker Amma Asante Responds to Claims Her WWII Drama 'Romanticizes Nazism'—TIFF," *Indiewire*, September 9, 2018, https://www.indiewire.com/2018/09/where-hands-touch-amma-asante-responds-social-media-1202001098/. Criticisms included observations about "taste" and the danger of humanizing the perpetrators which are familiar from generic debates about Holocaust representation.

ANTISEMITISM WARS: CHALLENGING THE AUTHORITY OF HOLOCAUST MEMORY

These new questions of mutual recognition *within* the Black diaspora are coinciding with a renewed crisis of mutual recognition between diasporic Blacks and Jews. In America, the strain of pessimism in thinking about "race" that was briefly interrupted by the "post-racial" moment with its ludic possibilities reaches back over a generation, to the disillusion that followed the murders of Martin Luther King and Malcom X, the criminalization and bloody suppression of radical Black activism and the progressive de-coupling of civil rights from social and economic justice programs in public policy. In the framing narrative of *Clifford's Blues*, the publisher who receives the protagonist's manuscript camp diary reflects that it is unlikely to be published because of a "severe generic problem in this business"—the problem of seeing Blacks and Holocaust in the same frame. The conjuncture of new knowledge about the Holocaust with the rise of an Afro-pessimist vision can explain the publication of *Clifford's Blues* in 1999, but in fact it was written in the 1980s, and has a clear affinity with Williams' dystopian works.[20] The protagonist of *The Book of Harlan*, having survived Buchenwald, lives through the downward spiral of urban Black communities in the 1970s and when he takes his revenge by murdering a former camp guard at the end of the novel, the redemption is a bitter one.

The moment of disappointment of the civil rights movement was also the moment of the unraveling in America of that historic alliance between Blacks and Jews, initially intensified by the Holocaust experience, that is invoked in Paul Gilroy's work of the 1990s and in Rothberg's *Multidirectional Memory*.[21] Rothberg and Gilroy were optimistic about the possibility that those solidarities could be realized again, once the material histories of common struggles were recalled. But by that time the prospects were already poor. Williams, whose wife was Jewish, signals solidarity by introducing *Clifford's Blues* with lines by Aimé Césaire that

---

[20] Bollinger, "Crimes"; Anthony C. Cooke, "Black Community, Media and Intellectual Paranoia-as-Politics," *Journal of Black Studies* 42, no. 4 (2011): 609–26.

[21] Paul Gilroy, *The Black Atlantic. Modernity and Double Consciousness* (London: Verso, 1993); Paul Gilroy, *Between Camps. Nations, Cultures and the Allure of Race* (Cambridge, MA: Belknap Press, 2000); Rothberg, *Multidirectional Memory*. See Eric J. Sundquist, *Strangers in the Land. Blacks, Jews, Post-Holocaust America* (Cambridge, MA: Belknap Press, 2005) for an analysis of the literary manifestations of the unraveling alliance.

invoke the two histories of slavery and oppression in the figure of the rivers of Babylon. But in a later interview he expressed impatience with forms of Jewish Holocaust piety that minimized the significance of the suffering of other victims.[22]

Claims for the primacy of Jewish victimhood gained new currency as the first decade of the twenty-first century waned. They are implicit in the ways in which Holocaust remembrance has become tied to celebration of the state of Israel in key public institutions. This nexus has been constructed over decades, but at a time when Israel was on the defensive against challenges to its moral and political legitimacy as a result of its occupation policies and domestic ethno-nationalism, its outcome was a new version of the hierarchical victim discourse that articulates moral authority in terms of Jews' privileged claim to victim status. For a period, at least, support for Israel as a principle became a precondition for moral and political legitimacy in public discourse, opening both specific criticism of Israel and talk of other victims (historical and contemporary) to charges of antisemitism.

These charges were actively deployed in political contests as the center fell away in the mid-2010s. In 2016, the British Labour Party under a new left-wing leadership became the main target of accusations of antisemitism. Challenged to resolve the problem by adopting the definition of antisemitism propagated by the International Holocaust Remembrance Alliance, the party was divided over the aspects of that definition which identify certain propositions about the state of Israel as examples of antisemitic speech. These include "denying the Jewish people their right to self-determination, e.g., by claiming that the existence of a State of Israel is a racist endeavor; applying double standards by requiring of it a behavior not expected or demanded of any other democratic nation; [and] drawing comparisons of contemporary Israeli policy to that of the Nazis" as well as "accusing Jewish citizens of being more loyal to Israel, or to the alleged priorities of Jews worldwide, than to the interests of their own nations [or] holding Jews collectively responsible for actions of the state of Israel."[23] Members of the party who, like party leader Jeremy Corbyn himself, were sympathetic to the situation of the Palestinians and critical to different degrees and in varying terms of Israeli policy perceived the terms of the

---

[22] Muller, Blaine and Bowen, "Clifford's Blues," 221.
[23] "Working Definition of Antisemitism," IHRA, accessed May 5, 2020, https://www.holocaustremembrance.com/node/196.

IHRA definition as inhibiting legitimate critical discussion of the past and present of the Middle East. The angry exchanges that ensued within the party and between the party and its critics, and which effectively set the leadership in opposition to the organized Jewish community in Britain as well as to many Jews within its own ranks, encompassed much more than the question of Israel, but the issue of mnemonic loyalty raised by the IHRA definition remained at its center.[24]

A particularly problematic aspect of the IHRA definition is the ban on comparisons in combination with the anticipated charge of "double standards." Implicitly reasserting the uniqueness of the Holocaust-as-Shoah, these provisions ignore the ways in which comparison between the crimes of the Nazis and other abuses, historical and contemporary, has become the currency of political rhetoric and also the object of scholarship. They also (paradoxically) limit the generalizability of the lessons of the Holocaust, which is part of the IHRA's mission. In the United States, these implications played themselves out during the summer of 2019 when Congresswoman Alexandria Ocasio-Cortez characterized the migrant detention camps on the US-Mexico border as concentration camps.[25] Amid the subsequent media storm, the United States Holocaust Memorial Museum (USHMM) felt obliged to issue a statement condemning all efforts to draw historical analogies with the Holocaust. Unsurprisingly, this provoked immediate protest from several hundred scholars and memory activists.[26]

The implications of this moment for mnemonic solidarity across racial divides was made clear by President Trump's attacks on Ocasio-Cortez and other Democratic congresswomen of color, attacks which linked their status as racialized immigrants, their socialist politics, their championing of immigrant rights and the imputation of antisemitism into a single charge of anti-Americanism. The charge of antisemitism, which did not

---

[24] The chronicle of these debates has yet to be written. The internal inquiry which was designed to resolve the question became an object of contention itself: Shami Chakrabarti, "The Shami Chakrabarti Inquiry," accessed May 5, 2020, https://labour.org.uk/wp-content/uploads/2017/10/Chakrabarti-Inquiry-Report-30June16.pdf.

[25] Sheryl Gay Stolberg, "Ocasio-Cortez calls migrant detention centers 'concentration camps,' eliciting backlash," *The New York Times*, June 18, 2019, https://www.nytimes.com/2019/06/18/us/politics/ocasio-cortez-cheney-detention-centers.html.

[26] Omer Bartov et al., "An Open Letter to the Director of the US Holocaust Memorial Museum." *New York Review of Books*, July 11, 2019, https://www.nybooks.com/daily/2019/07/01/an-open-letter-to-the-director-of-the-holocaust-memorial-museum.

originate with Trump but has been repeatedly deployed against them and other figures on the political and academic left, arises principally from their critique of Israeli policy, and in particular from their support for the campaign for Boycott, Disinvestment and Sanctions (BDS) against Israel. In December 2019, Trump issued an executive order which effectively redefined Judaism as a race or nationality. This made anti-Zionism (in the form of BDS) prosecutable under civil rights legislation, while at the same time declaring American Jews dual nationals with implicitly divided allegiance—diasporics in spite of themselves.[27] A particularly resonant example of the racial dimensions of the divide over BDS came when a civil rights organization in Alabama withdrew its offer of an award to the distinguished African-American philosopher and activist Angela Davis on the grounds of her support for BDS, apparently at the urging of a local Holocaust education group.[28]

Germany, too, was drawn into these "antisemitism wars" at the end of 2018. An anonymous communication to the German government, apparently of Israeli origin, accused a very large group of publicly financed NGOs of anti-Israeli bias in their support for Palestinian communities, their provision of platforms for speakers critical of Israel or their promotion of exhibitions that engage with historical and contemporary dimensions of Arab-Jewish relations in Israel.[29] In the wake of a Bundestag resolution of May 2019 affirming that the BDS movement is antisemitic, the director of the Jewish Museum in Berlin was forced to resign for expressing sympathy with BDS.[30] And in May 2020 several hundred writers, artists and scholars protested against the evidence that local authorities were pressuring event organizers and prize committees to withhold or withdraw awards to critics of Israeli policy. Precipitated by the anticipated "disinvitation" of Cameroonian writer Achille Mbembe by the

---

[27] Peter Baker and Maggie Haberman, "Trump targets anti-semitism and Israeli boycotts on college campuses," *The New York Times*, December 10, 2019, https://www.nytimes.com/2019/12/10/us/politics/trump-antisemitism-executive-order.html.

[28] The withdrawal was subsequently reversed: Niraj Chokshi, "Angela Davis won an award. It was revoked. Now it's been reinstated," *The New York Times*, January 25, 2019, https://www.nytimes.com/2019/01/25/us/angela-davis-israel.html.

[29] Jannis Hagmann, "Schwere Vorwürfe aus Israel," *Die Tageszeitung*, December 5, 2018, https://taz.de/Schreiben-liegt-der-taz-exklusiv-vor/!5553564/.

[30] Melissa Eddy, "Director of Berlin's Jewish Museum Quits After Spat Over B.D.S.," *The New York Times*, June 14, 2019, https://www.nytimes.com/2019/06/14/world/europe/berlin-jewish-museum-director-quits-bds.html.

Ruhrtriennale, their statement cited mainly artists and scholars of color as victims of this pressure.³¹

The storms of 2016–2020 were manifestly precipitated by a particular geopolitical conjuncture: Under the leadership of Benjamin Netanyahu, the Israeli state, which has always been active in promoting political sympathy in the diaspora, had intensified its counter-offensive against the negative public opinion generated by its policies. This was coupled in domestic policy with the creation of "facts on the ground" through the intensification of pressure on the populations of the occupied territories, the consolidation of the permanent status of settlements in defiance of international law, and constitutional changes aimed at redefining Israel as an ethno-national state. Netanyahu's ethno-nationalism in turn made him an ally of other national populist governments, including that of Donald Trump (an affinity potentiated by the unanticipated alliance of right-wing Zionism and the Christian evangelicalism). Similarly, Germany's Christian Democrat government was on the defensive as a result of pressure from a new ethno-nationalist right whose rhetorical target was now "Islam," although it remained a source of antisemitic violence in practice.

Accordingly, these events may prove to have been a hiccup in the progress of global knowledge and understanding of the Holocaust and its lessons. Even Kenneth Stern, the author of the IHRA's working definition of antisemitism, acknowledged the specificity of the moment in December 2019: "I drafted the definition of antisemitism. Right-wing Jews are weaponizing it."³² In spite of the contretemps over historical analogies, the USHMM, like all other institutions of Holocaust commemoration and education and the global community of Holocaust scholars, continues to acknowledge the full range of victim groups under the Nazis (all concentration camp inmates and victims of genocidal bio-politics) as subjects of Holocaust. And the question of comparability continues to be explored through the critical juxtaposing of the Holocaust with other genocides, even if its epochal character remains axiomatic in the very fact and acts of commemoration.

---

³¹ "Pledge opposing ideological or political interference and litmus tests in Germany," accessed May 15, 2020, https://nopoliticallitmustests.wordpress.com/pledge-opposing-ideological-or-political-interference-and-litmus-tests-in-germany/.

³² Kenneth Stern, "I drafted the definition of antisemitism. Right-wing Jews are weaponizing it," *The Guardian*, December 30, 2019, https://www.theguardian.com/commentisfree/2019/dec/13/antisemitism-executive-order-trump-chilling-effect?CMP.

Conversely, antisemitism is no chimera. The increase in publicly expressed hostility and violence against Jews in America and Europe is a real feature of the global rise of right-wing populism since the turn of the century. And in Britain, the harsh light shone on the Labour Party revealed that tropes and styles of thought and argument that are objectively antisemitic retain their currency and may be more easily tolerated than other forms of racism even among some who consider themselves progressive and anti-racist.[33]

Considered from the perspective of memory studies, though, this has something to tell us about the mutability of the meanings we attach to apperceptions of the past. Beyond opportunistic weaponizing, raising the specter of antisemitism works partly because of a real generational change in the shape of memory in the global North: Any claim to the uniqueness of the Holocaust and its message now contends with the voices of people for whom the Holocaust is not any kind of memory. In the British case, it has been argued that inattention to or trivialization of the reality and persistence of antisemitism was a consequence of the "drowning out" of postwar Holocaust consciousness after the 1960s, as racial justice was increasingly framed in terms of the claims of former colonial subjects.[34] And there is force in the argument of scholars close to the Labour Party debates that routinized anti-racism can neither recognize nor counter antisemitism as long as it uncritically positions Jews as "white."[35] In experiential terms, for Americans and Europeans with family histories of colonial oppression and violence, the sufferings of displaced and besieged Palestinians are more immediate than the historical trauma of Europe's Jews. And many of today's economic migrants and refugees are escaping situations in which the regional reverberations of the Arab-Israeli conflict and the great power contentions that underly it are a source of present distress. One result of this can be a lack of sensitivity to and even a new license for antisemitic language, imagery and actions in anti-imperialist and anti-capitalist discourse. Another result is that the charge of antisemitism is experienced as a silencing mechanism. In August 2018, 84 British Black and minority ethnic organizations published an open letter in which,

---

[33] Chakrabarti, *Inquiry*; Ben Gidley, Brian McGeever and David Feldman, "Labour and Antisemitism: a Crisis Misunderstood," *The Political Quarterly*, accessed May 15, 2020, https://doi.org/10.1111/1467-923X.12854.

[34] Andy Pearce, *Holocaust Consciousness in Contemporary Britain* (Oxford and New York: Routledge, 2014), 15 (citing John Solomos).

[35] Gidney, McGeever and Feldman, "Labour and Antisemitism."

invoking common histories of colonialism and racism, they insisted that freedom to choose the terms in which they comment on Israel was indivisible from the freedom to express their own needs and call for justice as minority communities in Britain.[36]

In the Jewish diaspora too, and among those non-Jews for whom Holocaust memory is foundational to political identity, the passage of time has wrought changes that make for irritable responses to the claims of new diasporic actors and may block impulses to solidarity. A form of political argumentation (from either side of the debate) that declares real world solidarity with Palestinians to be incompatible with mnemonic solidarity with the victims of the Holocaust tugs at a nexus of liberal sympathies that emerged in Germany, Britain and the United States after the Second World War, though with different timing and in different forms. In Germany, whose own Jewish Holocaust survivor population is negligible, the accusation that the German government was funding antisemitic activities touched a nerve because of the West German *state's* long-standing commitment to both material and moral support of Israel as part of its acknowledged responsibility to the victims of the Holocaust. At the level of civil society, the accusation was directed at cultural organizations whose agenda is the promotion of intercultural dialogue and also at charities whose engagement in projects in Africa and the Middle East can be seen as part of the legacy of German colonialism. While projects of this kind remain open to the charge of neo-colonialism, they have increasingly drawn their energy from critical reflection on that history, and even before that they were part of the formation of humanitarian globalism that, along with post-Holocaust philo-Semitism, underpinned West Germany's liberal consensus.[37]

The counter-charge, which (even when it falls short of direct analogies between Israel and Nazi Germany) positions supporters of Israel as complicit in practices of colonialism, racism and apartheid, exposes the

---

[36] "As BAME communities, we stand united against attempts to suppress our voices," *The Independent*, August 17, 2018, https://www.independent.co.uk/voices/letters/letters-ihra-definition-palestine-israel-bame-sexism-labour-denmark-a8496251.html.

[37] Carole Fink, *West Germany and Israel. Foreign Relations, Domestic Politics and the Cold War 1965–74* (Cambridge: Cambridge University Press, 2019); Britta Schilling, *Postcolonial Germany. Memories of Empire in a Decolonized Nation* (Oxford: Oxford University Press, 2014), 90–132; Claudia Olejniczak, *Die Dritte-Welt-Bewegung in Deutschland* (Wiesbaden: DUV, 1998), 75–6; Frank Stern, *The Whitewashing of the Yellow Badge. Antisemitism and Philosemitism in Postwar Germany* (Oxford: Pergamon, 1992).

instability of multidirectional memory. But it also challenges mnemonic investment in an imagined historical moment in which global acknowledgment of the Holocaust as a Jewish catastrophe was accompanied by a consensus in the West that the historical mission of the survivors was properly embodied in the new nation-state. It is well known that that "moment" was an extended one. Even in Israel it was not until the beginning of the 1960s that there crystallized a politically potent vision of the Holocaust legacy as one that called for honoring the victims as part of the process of Jewish identity construction.[38] In her chapter in this volume Carol Gluck reminds us of the importance of the 1961 Eichmann trial, which simultaneously brought the details of the Shoah to international attention and introduced Israel to the world as the champion of the survivors and other Jews in the diaspora, as well as of subsequent trials which extrapolated generic categories of crimes against humanity and commemorative justice from the Holocaust events. The adoption of the Holocaust as an identificatory point of reference for American Jews, and its entrance into the American cultural mainstream as "part of the language" (Peter Novick) was similarly the outcome of an extended chain of circumstances.[39] And Britain has had its own path to "Holocaust consciousness," the identity of British Jews informed by a high degree of assimilation in spite of endemic antisemitism and a relationship with empire complicated by British policy in Palestine since the Balfour Declaration of 1917. The fact that British Jews paid a price for the ambivalence of that policy in the riots in British cities that followed incidents of Jewish terrorism Palestine in 1947 is part of a community experience that underpins their tendency to identify more strongly with Israel than other European Jewish communities.[40]

As different as these national contexts were, they fed into a shared imaginative nexus that tied Israel's legitimacy to its status as the guardian

---

[38] Tom Segev, *The Seventh Million: The Israelis and the Holocaust*, trans. Heim Watzman (New York: Holt, 2000).

[39] Peter Novick, *The Holocaust in American Life* (New York: Houghton Mifflin, 1999); Henry L. Feingold, *Bearing Witness: How America and Its Jews Responded to the Holocaust* (Syracuse, NY: Syracuse University Press, 1995).

[40] Pearce, *Holocaust Consciousness*; Todd Endelman, *The Jews of Britain 1656–2000* (Berkeley/Los Angeles/London: University of California Press, 2002); Tony Kushner, "Anti-Semitism and austerity: the August 1947 riots in Britain," in *Racial Violence in Britain 1840–1950*, ed. Panikos Panayi (Leicester: Leicester University Press, 1993), 149–68.

of the moral legacy of the Holocaust victims.⁴¹ That vision of Israel and a narrative of origin that underlies it was also embedded in now-canonical media representations which reached global audiences. The film *Exodus*, released in 1960, which depicts the struggle for the creation of a Jewish state in postwar Palestine, went beyond the novel from which it was adapted in placing Holocaust survivors in key roles as well as in its focus on the theme of their rescue. It also introduced material not present in the novel which envisioned post-liberation Israel as a nation in which Jews and Arabs could live in harmony. And its liberal credentials—sanctioned at the time by the Israeli authorities that promoted it—were sealed by the involvement of blacklisted Communists, including screenwriter Dalton Trumbo, in its production.⁴² The 1978 television series *Holocaust*, which opened a new phase in popular awareness of the Holocaust especially in West Germany, ends with the arrival in Palestine of the young German Jewish survivor Rudi.⁴³ The closing scenes of *Schindler's List* (1993) make a similar mnemonic connection by taking the surviving Schindler Jews to Schindler's grave in Israel, and has clear resonances with the end of *Exodus*.⁴⁴

As *Exodus'* conciliationist conclusion testifies, this vision was not at its origin the work of the political right, just as there were strong socialist and secularist elements in the Israeli nation-building project. And from this point of view it is significant that it was not only Jews on the political right whose voices were raised in alarm and accusation during the antisemitism debates of 2016–2020. In Britain, those who would not associate themselves with the politics of the right (including Jews inside the Labour

---

⁴¹ Dan Diner, "Cumulative Contingency: Historicizing Legitimacy in Israeli Discourse," *History and Memory* 7, no. 1 (1995): 147–70.

⁴² M.M. Silver, *Our Exodus. Leon Uris and the Americanization of Israel's Founding Story* (Detroit: Wayne State University Press, 2010); Giora Goodman, "'Operation Exodus': Israeli government involvement in the production of Otto Preminger's Film *Exodus* (1960)," *The Journal of Israeli History* 33, no. 2 (2014): 209–29. See also Alan Mintz, *Popular Culture and the Shaping of Holocaust Memory in America* (Seattle: University of Washington Press, 2001), 3–35.

⁴³ *Holocaust* (NBC, Producers Robert Berger and Herbert Brodkin, 1978). The impact of the series in West Germany was explored in a special issue of *Historical Social Research/ Historische Sozialforschung* 30, no. 4 (2005).

⁴⁴ Cf Shai Ginsburg, "An American Reflection: Steven Spielberg, The Jewish Holocaust and the Israeli-Palestinian Conflict," *Miguk'ang* 34, no. 1 (2011): 45–76. Ginsburg proposes that these scenes in fact reflect Spielberg's skepticism about the failure of post-1967 Israel to fulfill the *Exodus* vision.

Party) were among the most sensitive to intimations of antisemitism associated with criticism of Israel and most militant in challenging them. This is in spite of the fact that while antisemitic speech and action by the non-establishment right were certainly increasing there, there was no evidence (by comparison with the United States) of its being endorsed by government, and surveys earlier in the decade showed that British Jews suffered less from antisemitic violence and were less afraid of it than Jews elsewhere in Europe.[45] Adapting Gilroy's language, I would suggest that among some diasporic Jews anxieties about antisemitism are fuelled by a post-Holocaust melancholia that draws on nostalgia for that moment which they remember as endowing Israel with the moral authority to act as a beacon for postwar moral reconstruction.

POPULATIONS IN MOTION AND THE UNRAVELING OF THE POSTWAR SETTLEMENT: DEFENDING "WHITE CHRISTIAN EUROPE"

Paul Gilroy is not the only critic to have anatomized the aporias of memory in Europe. Writing about France's memory culture, Ann Laura Stoler used the term "aphasia" to characterize the crippling incapacity of the postcolonial metropole to speak its past to itself.[46] In the Western cultural and medical tradition, melancholia and aphasia are pathologies. But in invoking these terms here is not my intention to pathologize the rememberers. The point, rather, is to pose the question (implicit in the term "aphasia") of what has remained unremembered, misremembered or actively suppressed in the mnemonic construction of an identificatory moment. This should make us attentive (with Gilroy) to the losses that have been incurred in this process—what we have to mourn and who is doing the mourning. Here it helps to take into account the ways in which remembered moments decay and are reconstructed as memory

---

[45] EU Agency for Fundamental Human Rights, *Experiences and perceptions of antisemitism Second survey on discrimination and hate crime against Jews in the EU* (Luxembourg: Publications Office of the European Union, 2018). Cf L. D. Staetsky and Jonathan Boyd, *The Exceptional Case? Perceptions and experiences of antisemitism among Jews in the United Kingdom* (London: Institute for Jewish Policy Research, 2014).

[46] Ann Laura Stoler, "Colonial Aphasia. Race and Disabled Histories in France," *Public Culture* 23, no. 1 (Winter 2011): 121–56.

communities are reshaped through the intervention of new rememberers—and also in resistance to those interventions.

In the case of the "antisemitism wars" the key driver at the level of mnemonic discourse is the global articulation of memories of the Nakba in forms that powerfully challenge the foundational myths of the state of Israel, which now include the Holocaust. That the challenge to Israel's *current* practices is often posed in the moral and rhetorical terms set in motion by the Holocaust and its aftermath appears paradoxical but is a logical consequence of that form of legitimation. But the historical moment in which the Arab-Israeli conflict emerged was the moment of a global postwar settlement, other aspects of whose legacy and memory are also now objects of contention. In 1947, India and Pakistan gained their independence. The year 1948 witnessed the United Nations Genocide Convention, which signaled the codification of a globally binding discourse of human rights in a self-conscious drawing of the lessons of the Holocaust.[47] It was also the year of (among other things) the Berlin conflict which initiated the division of Germany and with it the consolidation of the Cold War in Europe and of Communist hegemony in Eastern Europe, and (with the launch of the National Health Service) the beginning of Britain's experiment in social democracy. The ambivalences of that historical moment are many, but it resulted in a relatively stable discursive framework in which states and civil society groups deployed a shared language of internationalism, rights and justice. The rise of ethno-nationalism in Europe, America and Asia has been accompanied by an explicit rejection of that language along with the institutions that the postwar world community built to realize its promise.

In this volume, Jie-Hyun Lim points to the way in which official memory cultures were also stabilized, or frozen, in that postwar consensus, when he describes how new national victimhood narratives were "released" by the ending of the Cold War around 1990. He also alludes to the fact that in Europe—as in the Indian sub-continent and in Palestine—that postwar settlement rested on policies of partition and the forced displacement of populations (indeed, of re-settlement). The case of the expulsion of ethnic Germans from Eastern Europe to which Lim refers is exemplary in the way the vernacular memory of the events was alternately

---

[47] Samuel Moyn points out that the common view that "human rights" was a product of the postwar, post-Holocaust moment is itself a retrospective construct: *The Last Utopia. Human Rights in History* (Cambridge, MA and London: Harvard University Press, 2010).

instrumentalized and suppressed as the West German state negotiated its own relationship to the wartime and Holocaust past, to emerge after unification as part of a new narrative of German victimhood. But attention to this local example can distract from the ways in which traumas of this kind were experienced at the same time in many parts of Europe and its former colonies. We are reminded of this not least by the latest re-emergence of sources of conflict which partition and resettlement were intended to suppress, provoked and exploited by nationalist politicians who rely on selective memory and the mobilization of diasporic allegiance to legitimate their politics, whether in the Middle East or in the India of Narendra Modi.[48] (The case of Britain's welfare state is a reminder that postwar reconstruction also depended on large-scale labor migration, much of it from the colonies, which, like the "Windrush generation," is itself the object of complex practices of memory and forgetting.)

It is this aspect of the way the mnemonic nexus between colonialism, imperialism and the legacies of war and Holocaust is playing out in contemporary political contests that I want to address briefly here. I focus on Eastern European reactions to the twenty-first-century "refugee crisis" and the arrival in Europe of a new generation of displaced people. What is being remembered, what forgotten? Jie-Hyun Lim's account of Polish debates suggests that in the latest round of memory contests the Holocaust may be being displaced by colonialism as the hegemonic point of reference for victimhood claims: Poles not only disavow their own historical implication in colonialist practices when they declare dark-skinned refugees to be inherently alien to the Polish body politic, but they also claim moral authority as victims of great power colonialism.

Something else that has been officially forgotten in Eastern and Central Europe is the region's long history of ethnic and religious pluralism. The cohabitation of Muslims, Christians and Jews, Slavs, Italians, Magyars, Germans and Roma, in different combinations and often in the same communities, was a feature of this part of Europe before the First World War. Politically, it was institutionalized in the constitution of the Habsburg Empire, and the cosmopolitanism fostered, celebrated and constantly

---

[48] On the construction and mobilization of the "global Indian," see Varadarajan, *The Domestic Abroad*, 107–41. On the impacts of mobilization on South Asian communities and politics in Britain: Haroon Siddique, "'Divisive Tactics'," *The Guardian*, November 8, 2019, https://www.theguardian.com/politics/2019/nov/08/british-hindus-urged-whatsapp-messages-vote-against-labour.

re-negotiated by the institutions of empire survived in the successor states after its breakup. As Lim suggests, there were always hierarchical relationships and embedded practices of othering among ethnic and national groups, whether in partitioned Poland or the Habsburg Empire. And the record of irridentism, antisemitism and complicity with genocide in the states created by the 1919 peace treaties is nothing to celebrate.[49] In a very real sense, though, it was the Holocaust and the postwar settlement that produced ethnic homogeneity in the region.

There is thus a very particular mnemonic maneuver at work when nationalists in Poland, Hungary and Czechia invoke homogeneity as their natural heritage to legitimate their resistance to accepting refugees. In the rhetoric of Hungary's Fidesz government under Viktor Orbán, that resistance takes more militant form, as the closure of Hungary's borders to refugees is articulated as the front-line defense of a "white Christian Europe" against the invasion of an alien (i.e. Muslim) civilization. This structure of argument does have an authentic history, though it obfuscates the fact that Hungary was Europe's northernmost zone of contact with Islam and a conduit for Islamic culture until the late seventeenth century. Paired with the rhetoric of domestic defense against Jewish power, resurrected in Fidesz campaigns against George Soros and Western liberalism, it is part of the tradition of the Hungarian right, including the interwar antisemites whose legacy is being rehabilitated.

But in Hungary, returning to this interwar rhetoric means reaching back over genuinely formative (and traumatic) experiences of war, Holocaust and socialist reconstruction. And it is not accidental, but belongs to an extremely aggressive memory politics which is in some senses a study in paradoxes.[50] A central paradox is the elevation of the Treaty of Trianon to the status of foundational trauma, given that, following the principle of national self-determination, the treaty both established

---

[49] Johannes Feichtinger and Gary B. Cohen, eds., *Understanding Multiculturalism: The Habsburg Central European Experience* (New York and Oxford: Berghahn, 2015); Omer Bartov and Eric D. Weitz, eds., *Shatterzone of Empires. Coexistence and Violence in the German, Habsburg, Russian, and Ottoman Borderlands* (Bloomington and Indianapolis: Indiana University Press, 2013).

[50] Éva Kovács, "Overcoming History through Trauma: The Hungarian Historikerstreit," *European Review* 24, no. 4 (October 2016): 523–34. This website presents Trianon as a "grass-roots" movement with multiple local monuments: "Nekünk még legalább két-három Trianon kéne, de hamar!" Szily László, accessed May 7, 2020, https://cink.hu/nekunk-meg-legalabb-ket-harom-trianon-kene-de-hamar-1478546158.

Hungary as a nation state and made it more nearly ethnically homogeneous. What is mourned, of course, is the loss of territory which created Hungarian minorities in other successor states, and which went along with the loss of the dominion over other nationalities that Hungarians enjoyed as part of the dual monarchy. From this point of view, we might characterize the Eastern European rejection of cohabitation with refugees as an expression of (late) post-imperial melancholia: It reflects a selective memory of the historical past which is re-constituting the subjects of that history as an exclusive (memory) community and thereby blocking the possibility of solidarity—or even dialogue—among its heirs.

Conclusion: Memory Matters

Memory matters. Talking about the past is an eminently political act, and talking and writing critically about how people talk about the past engages our political instincts as well as the sinews of scholarship. This incurs hazards. The present volume would have included a fifth substantive chapter, had its author not been put in danger by police action against a memory activist whose work the chapter gestured at. The challenge at the level of scholarship is that the sense of the moment that makes particular memories matter, and the equally intuitive sense of how particular articulations of memory are working in the moment, may outrun the tools of scholarship: the sources, rhythms of critical reflection and structures of explanation that normally define our disciplines. To insist on the multidisciplinarity of memory studies is to acknowledge some of the tensions between the different ways in which we address "memory," between randomness and system, allusion and analysis, topography and explanation. As a historian, I feel some discomfort when I find myself making large statements in a small space and in discursive registers that may appear incommensurate, as I have here. It incurs an obligation to explain myself and to reflect on how to take critical analysis and praxis further.

The view that scholars are called on to respond to a general crisis of democratic values and practices as the second decade of the twenty-first century begins is widespread in memory studies as in the humanities more generally. My own sense of the moment and its implications for historical memory in Europe was galvanized by my experiences in the summer of 2018, during the first engagements of what I refer here to as the antisemitism wars. I felt its force in the course of my own memory work in Liverpool, a proudly multicultural city with strong and fiercely politicized memory cultures, when I was party to two accusations of antisemitism. The first was directed at me. I had curated an exhibition on the persecution of German Sinti and Roma, and wanted to follow it up with an event about the rather different experience of Romanian Roma which would provide an opportunity for dialogue between Jewish survivors and their children and immigrant Roma. The use of the term "Holocaust" to characterize the genocide of Roma and Sinti in the publicity for the event led to protest from a member of the host organization. The protest asserted the historical and moral uniqueness of the Shoah; the social media context in which it was raised situated it in the militant campaign against antisemitism.

In the second case I was made aware of an accusation of antisemitism leveled against an exhibition co-curated by a colleague. The exhibition's central theme was the historical relationship between transatlantic slavery, colonialism and luxury consumption—issues central to Liverpool's civic memory politics which have also engaged my scholarly attention. All of the works on display were by British artists the Singh Twins. The image that attracted the charge of antisemitism was one displayed to complement the main exhibition. Entitled *Partition Politics—Business as Usual*, it offers a conspectus of partitions carried out by colonial powers, exploited by international capital, and contested by non-state actors. Images of the occupied West Bank are at the center of a design that also refers to the Scramble for Africa, the partition of India and the Western intervention in Suez, foregrounding the international arms trade as driver and beneficiary of regional conflicts. After taking advice, the gallery managers rejected the claim of antisemitism. However, while the picture remained, the gallery felt obliged to post a disclaimer at the exhibition entrance.[51]

In that moment the unanticipated resonances of my public engagement with the Holocaust's "other victims" encroached on my more scholarly project of the moment: puzzling out the meanings of Black Holocaust fictions. I was positioned in spite of myself in a memory war. I originally entitled this chapter "Mnemonic Knots," a pessimistic riff on

---

[51] The image is reproduced in Eve Rosenhaft, "Europe's Melancholias and the Crisis of Multidirectional Memory," *global-e* 12, no. 8 (2019), accessed May 15, 2020, https://www.21global.ucsb.edu/global-e/february-2019/europe-s-melancholias-and-crisis-multidirectional-memory.

the notion of "entangled memories." Here, I have focused largely on the skeptical dimension of the mnemonic solidarity project, mapping a form of internal "re-territorialization" of memory. This process has manifestly been promoted and energized by the rise of the political right across the globe. But the affective power of these interventions and the discourses they have released invites us to ask how the identities of the contending groups are invested in the ways in which the past is remembered. Here, I suggest that attention to the nexus of Holocaust and postwar reconstruction as an object of both remembering and forgetting can be productive, given that it is the discourses of human rights and internationalism that emerged out of that moment that are under attack in this century. The double-edged character of the mnemonic moment is apparent in the deployment of accusations of antisemitism that draw their authority from Holocaust memory by the very politicians who are challenging the postwar settlement and promoting active racism and antisemitism at home. And the anxieties precipitated by these destabilizing contradictions are real, particularly, I argue, for those who were shaped in one way or another by the postwar moment (among whom I count myself). This is where the different subject positions (and histories) represented by dwellers in the global North become relevant, and I suggest that the effects of both migration and generational change are at work in the fracturing and reconfiguring of memory communities, both national and global-diasporic. These remain intuitions and hypotheses that invite further exploration.

Such exploration would also need to take account the epochal shifts in the political economy of the global North that have taken place since 1945 (and that have also impacted the global South). The postwar social settlement was unraveling in the West well before the collapse of socialism in the East, to be replaced by neo-liberal regimes of varying reach and intensity. From this point of view, the celebration of Britain's National Health Service—in the costumes and imagery of 1948—that formed the centerpiece of the opening of the 2012 Olympic Games in London is no less surprising in its timing than Orbán's mourning of Trianon. It is perfectly clear that in both the East and the West of the global North, populism and xenophobia reflect the hurts incurred by neo-liberal economic policies. Less clear is how the ways in which people refer to the past in interpreting those hurts have been shaped by the dynamics of the economic system. One result of the collapse of socialism and the triumph of neo-liberalism was the de-legitimizing of the labor movement and its memories, and this may have contributed to the framing of Holocaust in terms that valorize victimhood. Reflecting on the dialectics of race and diaspora, critics of the paradigm of multiculturalism have pointed to the roots in consumerist individualism—the neo-liberal personality—which it shares with certain kinds of identity politics that are in permanent tension with a progressive politics of memory and practical solidarity.[52] This essay has focused on imagined pasts. A further thinking through of the present mnemonic moment would need to take into account the impact of profound changes at the level of political economy, not only on structures of sentiment and expectation but also on the communicability of material pasts—experiences and aspirations.

There is, of course, a note of pessimism in my use of the term "melancholia" to denote some ways in which the selective memory of a complex history impinges on perceptions and action in the present. With Paul Gilroy, I apply it to histories that have made the global North what it is: colonialism, continental imperialism and the Holocaust foundations of both human rights discourse and the statehood of Israel. I use it not in an accusatory spirit, but to signal the tenderness of memory that makes it susceptible to shock and pain when other people's experiences of the shared past insist on being heard.

This is where the optimistic dimension of the mnemonic solidarity project comes in. The encounter between Jewish and Roma survivors that I was organizing in the summer of 2018 went ahead (with re-worded publicity) and led to a powerful exchange, new kinds of mutual recognition and continuing collaborations. In the context of my exhibition work, too, I have learned the importance of face-to-face encounters. Conversations with and between Jewish and Roma Holocaust survivors—too often contenders in a hierarchy of victimhood—confirm the potential of vernacular memory for generosity. But my exhibition experience has also taught me how important it is that those conversations are informed by a shared store of knowledge about each others' history, a level plane of understanding that enables recognition and the negotiation of difference.[53] Providing

[52] See, for example, Rey Chow, *The Protestant Ethnic and the Spirit of Capitalism* (New York: Columbia University Press, 2002), 102–18. I am grateful to Ian Gwinn for provoking me to these reflections.

[53] Kyu Dong Lee and Eve Rosenhaft, "Roma/Holocaust/Representation. Exhibition Experiences on Two Continents," *Critical Romani Studies*, forthcoming 2021.

that information and ensuring that it is received is one of the jobs of scholars. Scholarship and activism together will do best to link such grass roots conversations to critiques of the discourses of national and community *ressentiment* that constrain empathy and the social and geopolitical practices of power that persistently force us into adversarial positions—"partition politics" in the widest sense.

Open Access This chapter is licensed under the terms of the Creative Commons Attribution 4.0 International License (http://creativecommons.org/licenses/by/4.0/), which permits use, sharing, adaptation, distribution and reproduction in any medium or format, as long as you give appropriate credit to the original author(s) and the source, provide a link to the Creative Commons licence and indicate if changes were made.

The images or other third party material in this chapter are included in the chapter's Creative Commons licence, unless indicated otherwise in a credit line to the material. If material is not included in the chapter's Creative Commons licence and your intended use is not permitted by statutory regulation or exceeds the permitted use, you will need to obtain permission directly from the copyright holder.

CHAPTER 4

What the World Owes the Comfort Women

Carol Gluck

Fig. 4.1 Comfort Woman statue in Seoul (Carol Gluck)

C. Gluck (✉)
Weatherhead East Asian Institute, Columbia University, New York, NY, USA
e-mail: cg9@columbia.edu

© The Author(s) 2021
J.-H. Lim, E. Rosenhaft (eds.), *Mnemonic Solidarity*, Entangled Memories in the Global South,
https://doi.org/10.1007/978-3-030-57669-1_4

Abstract The women who served in Japan's military brothels across Asia during the Second World War are a focus of the politics of memory in East Asia as well as a touchstone for international human rights and sexual violence against women. By the 1990s, the "comfort women" had become a "traveling trope," which like the Holocaust, both recognized and transcended its original time and place. Gluck traces their "coming into memory" through changes in five areas of the evolving postwar "global memory culture": law, testimony, rights, politics, and notions of responsibility. She shows how the ideas and practices of public memory changed over time, in the course of which the comfort women became "global victims" in a transnational memoryscape.

Keywords World War II • Comfort women • Public memory • Testimony • Global memory culture • Japan; Korea

In 2015, during the year of the seventieth anniversary of the end of the Second World War, the politics of memory in East Asia bristled with tension. The strong rhetoric and diplomatic sparring arose in the context of surging nationalisms in an ecology of public memory that since the 1990s had once again employed history as a political instrument to arouse patriotism, promote national unity, and strengthen support for the regime in power. This global phenomenon included such political leaders as Abe Shinzō in Japan, Vladimir Putin in Russia, Xi Jinping in China, Narendra Modi in India, Recep Tayyip Erdoğan in Turkey, Viktor Orbán in Hungary, and a number of others who played the national history card for domestic purposes and then deployed it in international relations.

For East Asia, Russia, and Eastern Europe, World War II remained a magnetic site of memory in the polarized landscape of instrumental nationalism. No surprise then that the seventieth anniversary of the end of the war, like the fiftieth and sixtieth before it, generated a geopolitical blizzard of angry interchanges among East Asian leaders, with others, including Americans and Germans, adding their voices in an effort to calm the latest historical storms in the region. What might have been surprising, however, was the way in which the "comfort women," who served the Japanese military in brothels throughout wartime East and Southeast Asia, occupied so central a place in the geopolitics of memory in 2015. Ten years earlier in 2005, the sixtieth anniversary of the end of the war, the comfort women had figured in diplomatic tensions with South Korea, and

China together with protests against Japanese history textbooks and politicians' visit to Yasukuni, the national shrine of the war dead. In that year conservative Prime Minister Koizumi repeated the general apology for Japan's having "caused tremendous damage and suffering to the people of many countries" that had been offered for the first time by socialist Prime Minister Murayama on the fiftieth anniversary in 1995. In 1995, the comfort women had indeed been a prominent government issue. Following a direct apology to former comfort women by a cabinet official in 1993 (the Kōno Statement), Prime Minister Murayama established the quasi-official Asian Women's Fund to compensate survivors, inaugurating a controversial "Atonement Project," which began in 1995 and ended in 2007.[1]

Outside official circles in the public terrain of war memory, the former comfort women remained a vexed and visible presence for the remainder of the 1990s, as Chinese and South Korean leaders chastised Japan for not having confronted what they called its "history problem." Yet in most Asian countries the continued and expanded efforts to recognize and compensate the surviving comfort women took place in civil society, largely apart from the state. How then did the comfort women come to the fore in 2015 as a target of renewed government denial in Japan; a sharpened diplomatic weapon in South Korea, even overshadowing for a moment the ever sore point of Japanese colonial rule; an issue evoked in China together with the Nanjing Massacre and other wartime atrocities; a talking point for both South Korea and China in the controversies with Japan over the disputed islands in East Asian waters? One answer lay in the rising tide of nationalism in Japan, China, and South Korea, which threatened to sweep away earlier signs of transnational reconciliation and recreate the hostilities of decades past. Yet, when it came to the comfort women, no amount of nationalistic flag-waving and geopolitical name-calling was likely to alter the views of wartime violence against women that had spread

---

[1] "Statement by Prime Minister Junichirō Koizumi," Ministry of Foreign Affairs of Japan, August 15, 2005, accessed May 3, 2020, http://www.mofa.go.jp/announce/announce/2005/8/0815.html; "Statement by Prime Minister Murayama 'On the occasion of the 50th anniversary of the war's end'(August 15 1995)," Ministry of Foreign Affairs of Japan, August 15, 1995, accessed May 16, 2020, https://www.mofa.go.jp/announce/press/pm/murayama/9508.html; "Statement by the Chief Cabinet Secretary Yōhei Kōno on the result of the study on the issue of "comfort women"," Ministry of Foreign Affairs of Japan, August 4, 1993, accessed May 3, 2020, www.mofa.go.jp/policy/women/fund/state9308.html; "Closing of the Asian Women's fund," Asian Women's Fund, accessed May 3, 2020, www.awf.or.jp/e3/dissolution.html.

so widely during the preceding two decades. Nor would renewed Japanese denials of coercion be likely to dissuade international opinion from focusing on the injustice of the comfort women system.

The reasons for these predictions, I argue, are to be found in the changes that occurred in the ideas and practices of public memory in the second half of the twentieth century, often as a result of the conflicted processes of remembering the Second World War. Identifying five areas in what I call the *global memory culture* that evolved, largely since 1945, I suggest the ways in which the comfort women figured in each of them. The areas are *law*, changes in the legal processes treating past injustice; *testimony*, changes in the ways we know the past; *rights*, changes in notions of the obligations states and societies owe their citizens in relation to history; *politics*, changes in national and international political practice in regard to historical wrongs; and *responsibility*, changes in ideas of moral accountability for past and present actions. Entangled with one another in social practice and crossing national borders in influence and impact, these trends amounted to a sea change in the ideas of how the past is—or ought to be—collectively and publicly remembered.

LAW: CHANGES IN JUDICIAL PROCESS

Legal changes linked to the war occurred in both criminal and civil law. In criminal trials, the main trends over time included the change from a focus on perpetrators to a focus on victims; from conventional war crimes to crimes against humanity; and from legal locality to universal jurisdiction. This began of course with the Nuremberg and Tokyo War Crimes Tribunals held in Germany and Japan immediately after the war. Following conventional judicial procedure, the Allied trials assigned individual responsibility for the newly defined crimes against peace and crimes against humanity. The trial of wartime leaders had another, overtly pedagogical, goal of offering history lessons for "civilization," which according to Justice Robert Jackson was "the real complaining party" at the bar in Nuremberg.[2] Thus the trials were in part *performative justice:* in this case, performing the consequences of the deeds of Nazi and Japanese officials in waging barbaric and aggressive war. The trial of the Class A war crimi-

---

[2] "Opening Statement before the International Military Tribunal," Robert H. Jackson Center, accessed May 16, 2020, https://www.robertjackson.org/speech-and-writing/opening-statement-before-the-international-military-tribunal/.

nals in Tokyo had the *memory effect* of seeming to hold twenty-eight leaders responsible for the war while everyone else—emperor and people included—could imagine themselves as their victims.

The comfort women—or "comfort girls," as American wartime reports referred to them—were not included in the Allied charges. They were not purposely excluded, like the biological war crimes of the Japanese army's research Unit 731, but in part because of what might be called "familiarity blindness." At that time, and afterward too, brothels were familiar, considered normal or necessary by a number of militaries to protect troops against venereal disease and local populations against rape. Thus although Dutch, French, and Chinese investigators presented evidence of Japanese sexual violence, it seems plausible that the comfort women system itself was not "seen" as an ethical or criminal violation: that prosecutors were as if morally "blind" to it. An exception occurred later in the so-called B-C Trials for conventional war crimes conducted by nine Allies in seven Asian countries with more than six-thousand defendants, large numbers of them charged with mistreating Allied POWs. In one such Dutch trial in Batavia in the Indies, Japanese officers were tried and convicted for "forced prostitution" of thirty-five Dutch women, a charge that derived as much from the violation of racial as of gender boundaries. In terms of public memory, the many tens of thousands of Asian comfort women remained invisible, or at least unseen, in the charges made at the postwar tribunals.[3]

However flawed the legal bases of the "victors' justice" meted out at Nuremberg and Tokyo, the tribunals set the course for developing criteria and procedures for adjudicating violations of evolving international law. By the 1990s, in the International Criminal Courts for the former Yugoslavia and Rwanda, crimes against humanity had become central; and international legal tribunals—if still, as ever, beset with legal difficulties—had become an established means of post-conflict practice. This change occurred, not only through international law proper but through substantial changes in national courts, primarily in trials related to the Holocaust. These national trials were also *performative* and pedagogical in intent, but

---

[3] The numbers given vary from more than 200,000, the figure commonly used by international scholars and activists, to between 20,000 and 40,000, a number associated with historian Hata Ikuhiko and echoed by conservative Japanese "denialists." See Hata Ikuhiko, *Ianfu to senjō no sei* (Tokyo: Shinchōsha, 1999). Chances are that some 100,000 women were involved, although in my view the exact number, while ultimately unknown, matters less than the brute fact of the extent of the "comfort women system."

their practice—and memory effect—changed over time, until victims became almost as central as perpetrators.

Many identify a turning point in the 1961 Eichmann Trial in Jerusalem, which brought victims' stories directly into the Israeli courtroom in testimonies of survivors, including the pseudonymous Kazetnik "of the planet of Auschwitz."[4] The testimonies continued in the 1963–65 trials of the Auschwitz guards in West German courts, which while conducted under German criminal law helped to spread knowledge of the Holocaust more widely, shifting the weight of wartime criminality toward an emphasis on crimes against humanity. In France, after the 1970s, the national obsession with the Vichy past intersected over time with the increasing prominence of Holocaust memory. By the late 1990s, in the trial of Maurice Papon for his role in the wartime deportation of Jews, the testimonies of family members and the photographs of victims projected on the courtroom walls made the trial into a form of what some have called *commemorative justice*.[5] Before the long tail of Holocaust justice reached its end as the last perpetrators died, the trials in national courts had helped over the years to alter the script of war crimes adjudication. Other official, quasi-judicial procedures developed that paid similar attention to the importance of victims' stories, in particular, modes of transitional justice like Truth and Reconciliation Commissions, which performed the past for the sake of recognition of grievous wrongs in Latin America, South Africa, and elsewhere. Often cloaked as much in moral as in legal authority, these commissions attempted to provide a kind of *restorative justice*, whose aim was to heal society, not leave it forever divided into victims on one side and perpetrators on the other.

These altered national scripts of memory politics had significant effects on international law, including, for example, the assertion of universal jurisdiction in the form of the end of legal impunity for heads of state, as represented by the case of the Chilean dictator Augusto Pinochet in 1998–2000. Transnational discourses on human rights led to the inclusion of rape as a crime against humanity in the Rome Statute of the

---

[4] His real name was Yehiel Dinur, though he later became famous as Kazetnik, "inmate of a concentration camp." For part of his testimony (Sessions 68, 69), see The Nizkor Project, accessed May 4, 2020, http://www.nizkor.com/ftp.cgi/people/e/eichmann.adolf/transcripts/Sessions.

[5] Nancy Wood, "The Papon Trial in an 'Era of Testimony'," in *The Papon Affair: Memory and Justice on Trial*, ed. Richard L. Golsan (London: Routledge, 2000), 96–114 (here 96–97).

International Criminal Court in 1998. In each phase of the numerous legal justifications for this landmark statute, the arguments referred to the "Asian comfort women," who had raised their voices in public at around the same time in the early 1990s that Bosnian "rape camps" and women's rights—or as it was then expressed, the human rights of women—drew the international spotlight. Just as the Holocaust became a global example of genocide, so did the comfort women become a touchstone for new international law relating to the violence against women in war. And so rape, a violation as old as warfare itself, became a crime against humanity in international law. The first conviction for employing rape as a weapon of war occurred in the International Criminal Tribunal for the Former Yugoslavia in The Hague in 2001.[6]

The second area of legal change relating to World War II appeared in the increasingly important civil trials, which adjudicated claims filed by individuals or by groups in class-action suits, for redress, restitution, and compensation for grievances suffered during the war. The demands concerned compensation for individuals, as distinguished from reparations exacted between states. Moreover, these individuals or groups were not only suing their own governments, they were also making direct legal claims against foreign states and foreign corporations. And they frequently did so without the assistance of their national governments, or even in the face of state opposition. Amid the surge of civil suits during the 1990s, many related to the Holocaust, the comfort women, too, went to court. Indeed, the 1991 class-action lawsuit filed by three Korean former comfort women and others against the Japanese government accelerated the process of the comfort women *coming into memory* in the broader public landscape of views of the wartime past.

Their existence, after all, had never been a secret in Japan. The comfort women appeared in newspapers, novels, films, nonfiction accounts, and in parliamentary discussion about the relief law for former Japanese comfort women.[7] Nonetheless, somewhat like the impact of the Holocaust survivor testimonies at the Eichmann trial, the initial civil suit and public

---

[6] For this and other cases of rape in international courts, see Mark Ellis, "Breaking the Silence: Rape as an International Crime," *Case Western Reserve Journal of International Law* 38, no. 2 (2006–7): 225–47.

[7] For the Diet questioning about relief for former Japanese comfort women, Ikeya Kōji, "'Ianfu'engo jitsurei ni kansuru kokkai shingi," *Sensō sekinin kenkyū* 33 (Autumn 2001): 76–81.

statements by the Korean women in 1991 made the comfort women *visible* to a wider public. In this and subsequent suits Japanese courts routinely denied the plaintiffs' claims, basing their denial on earlier state-to-state treaties, such as the one concluded between Japan and South Korea in 1965; the lack of provision in international law for claims by individuals; or the statute of limitations, which for civil suits in Japan was twenty years. Yet, as Japanese courts continued to rule against the plaintiffs for damages, the introductory narratives and appendices of the negative judgments began to acknowledge violations of international law, coercion, suffering and even the responsibility (but not the obligation) of the government to recognize them. In suits filed by Korean, Filipino, Chinese, Taiwanese, and Dutch women, the courts rejected compensation, but a number of judges recognized the truthfulness, the "irrefutable historical evidence," of the plaintiffs' accounts of abduction, brutality, and violence.[8] The *compensatory, or reparative, justice* denied in these failed lawsuits nonetheless reflected and affected the changing public memory of the comfort women in Japan and around the world.

Yet it is clear that criminal and civil trials are imperfect vehicles for dispensing justice on matters like war responsibility and wartime sexual violence, not least because the law is not designed to put history on trial. Rules of evidence, burdens of precedent, and the generally conservative character of legal systems limit what national and international courts can do, even when they are so minded. Still, it is true that the body of international law accumulated since the end of World War II contributed to what one scholar termed "trans-temporal justice," and others refer to as "memory-justice."[9] In their *performative, commemorative, restorative, and compensatory* roles, the criminal and civil trials helped to change the law and also the way in which the darkest parts of the past were regarded. They had, in short, a powerful memory effect.

---

[8] Tsubokawa Hiroko and Ōmori Noriko, *Shihō ga nintei shita Nihongun "ianfu": higaikagai jijitsu wa kesenai!* (Kyoto: Kamogawa shuppan, 2011).
[9] Kohki Abe. "International Law as Memorial Sites: The Comfort Women Lawsuits Revisited," *Korean Journal of International and Comparative Law* 1, no. 2 (2013): 166–87 (here 181–82); Christopher J. Piranio and Edward Kanterian, "Memory, Justice and the Court: On the Dimensions of Memory-Justice under the Rome Statute," *Cambridge Review of International Affairs* 24, no. 3 (2011): 425–47.

Testimony: Changes in the Way We Know the Past

The second area of change is epistemological, a result of the expanded role of testimony as a window on history. We live, one French historian said, in "the era of the witness," epitomized by the 1990s, when individual testimonies of personal wartime experience overflowed the courtroom, the memoir, and social memory circles to become one of the main currencies of public memory and an increasingly recognized source of knowledge about the past.[10] In many instances the signal importance of witnessing had to do with the nature of the crimes and injustices at issue. They were often not documented, not recorded, not written down, and indeed in many cases, they were actively covered up, the evidence of their existence destroyed or expunged. This was as true of state crimes against the Disappeared in Latin America in the 1970s as of the civil violence of the Rwandan genocide in the 1990s. The deportation of the Jews of Western Europe and the extermination camps to which they were sent were indeed documented, sometimes in horrifying detail. But the so-called Holocaust by bullets in Eastern Europe, in which millions of Jews were killed in mass shootings, left mostly traces of mass graves and ghostly villages as evidence of its murderous horror.[11] How often it happened during the massacres of civilians, which occurred in so many regions during World War II, that there was "just one witness," frequently someone who had climbed out from under a pile of corpses as the sole survivor of the mass murder that took place on that spot.[12] The question then became: Was just one witness sufficient to know the truth of what happened there? Or, to use the language of a common challenge to the value of oral testimony, whether made near to the events or at a great distance of time: No documents, no historical truth. This modern conceit, so long established and so deeply believed—that history must be derived from written sources—came in fact to be regarded differently in the era of the witness than it was in earlier years. The voices of the victims had been heard. Testimonies of Holocaust

---

[10] Annette Wieviorka, *The Era of the Witness* (Ithaca, NY: Cornell University Press, 2006).
[11] See Patrick Desbois, *The Holocaust by Bullets: A Priest's Journey to Uncover the Truth Behind the Murder of 1.5 Million Jews* (New York: Palgrave Macmillan, 2008); Timothy Snyder, *Bloodlands: Europe Between Hitler and Stalin* (New York: Basic Books, 2010).
[12] Carlo Ginzburg, "Just One Witness," in *Probing the Limits of Representation: Nazism and the "Final Solution"*, ed. Saul Friedländer (Cambridge, MA: Harvard University Press, 1992), 82–96. Ginzburg's context is different but the Roman formulation of "one witness, no witness" presents the same legal problem here.

survivors now numbered in the tens of thousands, joined by those of others who suffered in, or suffered through, the war.[13] Ordinary people, most of them, their voices were supplemented at times by those of equally ordinary perpetrators, not concentration camp commandants but Polish villagers, not military leaders in Tokyo but soldiers who used the comfort stations in Asia. These testimonies raised the epistemological challenge of how to know the past in order to do justice to it.

There is no doubt that the testimonies of former comfort women proved crucial in the process of their coming into public memory.[14] After 1991, when Kim Hak-sun, the first Korean comfort woman to tell her story publicly, appeared in South Korean and Japanese media, the gathering of witnesses, oral histories, interviews, and testimonies across Asia gradually amassed a powerful archive of overlapping accounts of comfort women who served the imperial Japanese military throughout its areas of wartime occupation. These by then elderly women told of brutality and horror about which many had long remained silent—out of trauma, shame, or survival instinct. They were now old enough to tell their stories and to want their stories heard. And in a late twentieth-century social context altered by feminism, women's rights, concerns about sexual violence, and local, regional, and global challenges to the deficits in Japan's war memory, there were people willing to listen to them and to help them seek justice so long deferred. "I want to shake the whole world," said one former Korean comfort woman, and together with others who recounted their experiences, shake the world they did.[15] The public power of private stories proved enormous. In the Women's International War Crimes Tribunal, held in Tokyo in 2000 as a "people's tribunal" on Japanese mili-

---

[13] For example, the 55,000 video testimonies in the Visual History Archive of the USC Shoah Foundation, which began as a Holocaust archive but expanded to other genocides, in which it includes the Nanjing Massacre, https://sfi.usc.edu/.

[14] Although for the sake of simplicity I refer to the former comfort women, it is important to stress that they were aided, supported, and funded by a transnational network of activists and civil organizations throughout their efforts to obtain redress. Stephanie Wolfe notes this difference from Japanese-American and Jewish redress movements: *The Politics of Reparations and Apologies* (New York: Springer-Verlag, 2013), 245.

[15] "Shake the whole world": Hwang Koom Ja in the documentary film by Dai Sil Kim-Gibson, *Silence Broken: Korean Comfort Women* (see her book with the same title (Parkersburg, IA: Mid-Prairie Books, 1999). The documentary includes testimonies of soldiers as well as comfort women. See also the documentary *Shusenjo: The Main Battleground of the Comfort Women Issue* by Miki Dezaki (2018), which includes comments from all sides, including deniers.

tary sex slavery with international prosecutors and judges, nearly seventy former comfort women attended, twenty of whom told their stories as witnesses before the mock tribunal.[16] Coming from nine countries, including East Timor and North Korea, most of them did not know one another, and many had never spoken publicly (or even privately) of what they had suffered. Two former Japanese soldiers testified, too, but it was the women whose stories made the tribunal a testament to a still largely unrecorded history.

The reasons for this are well known. Rape and sexual violence are among the most difficult experiences to trace, or even talk about, especially for their female victims, whether in peacetime or in war. In addition, it appears that there was no extensive documentation of the comfort women system, and much of what might have existed was either destroyed or did not survive the end of the war. That the imperial Japanese army established or encouraged military brothels was clear from documentary evidence unearthed by the historian Yoshimi Yoshiaki in 1992, after the three Korean former comfort women came forward with their stories.[17] Japanese military brothels—the "comfort women system"—were part of a sprawling, far-flung, and diverse operation that ranged from the Philippines in the Pacific to the Nicobar Islands in the Indian Ocean, but it was one that did not leave much of a paper trail. What it did leave was human evidence in the testimonies of the former comfort women, which provided accounts of systematic violations of human rights.

Abe Shinzō, Diet member and twice prime minister, held a different view Elected to the Diet in 1993, he campaigned with conservative allies

---

[16] Some testified on video, some in person. For the 2001 judgment, which found the Japanese government guilty of crimes against humanity in "state-sanctioned rape and enslavemen," see "The Prosecutors and the Peoples of the Asia-Pacific Region v. Hirohito Emperor Showa et al.," International Crimes Database, accessed May 16, 2020, http://www.internationalcrimesdatabase.org/Case/981/The-Prosecutors-and-the-Peoples-of-the-Asia%E2%80%93Pacific-Region/. For testimonies of former Chinese comfort women, See Peipei Qiu, Su Zhuliang and Chen Lifei, *Chinese Comfort Women: Testimonies from Imperial Japan's Sex Slaves* (Vancouver: University of British Columbia Press, 2013).

[17] Yoshimi Yoshiaki became a central scholar and activist in the movement for redress for the comfort women and recognition of state responsibility for the wartime system of sex slavery. *Jūgun ianfu shiryōshū* (Tokyo: Ōtsuki shoten, 1992); *Jūgun ianfu* (Tokyo: Iwanami shoten, 1995). In English: Yoshimi Yoshiaki, *Comfort Women: Sexual Slavery in the Japanese Military During World War II*, trans. Suzanne O'Brien (New York: Columbia University Press, 2000); Yoshimi Yoshiaki, *Kaishun suru teikoku: Nihongun ianfu mondai no kitei* (Tokyo: Iwanami shoten, 2019).

against what they called "masochistic history" in the late 1990s.[18] As prime minister in 2006–07, Abe denied that the comfort women had suffered "coercion in any narrow sense"—something that his own party had admitted in the 1993 Kōno statement—since nothing "in the documents" confirmed such a view.[19] Then, more aggressively in his second term as prime minister beginning in late 2012, Abe made the comfort women a focus in the run-up to the seventieth anniversary of the end of the war in 2015. He commissioned a report intended to discredit the Kōno statement and continued to deny what he called the "baseless, slanderous claims" of sexual slavery and the forcible taking (*kyōsei renkō*, forced labor) of women.[20] Instead, the comfort women were prostitutes who voluntarily signed up, young women duped by Korean or Chinese civilian recruiters, or daughters either sold by their parents or driven by poverty to sell themselves. While women of these backgrounds could be found in the brothels, so, too, were young girls forcibly taken and forcibly prevented from escaping the brutal physical treatment to which many were later subjected. To make the argument against coercion—and the national dishonor associated with trafficking and sex slavery—the government and its nationalistic supporters denigrated the testimonies of the former comfort women as—in their words—subjective, inconsistent, nebulous, unreliable, and as just

---

[18] Masochistic (*jigyakuteki*) history was associated with the revisionist *jiyūshugi shikan* (liberal view of history) founded by Fujioka Nobukatsu in 1995 and with the Atarashii rekishi kyōkasho o tsukuru kai [Society for History Textbook Reform], formed in 1996. Abe was the secretary of the Young Diet Members Group for Japan's Future and History Education, established in 1997, supporting the revisionist textbooks and countering the recent public accounts of the comfort women. For a summary of the range of right-wing revisionism, see Sven Saaler, "Nationalism and History in Contemporary Japan," *The Asia-Pacific Journal-Japan Focus* 14, issue 20, no. 7 (October 2016): 1–17, https://apjjf.org/2016/20/Saaler.html.

[19] Abe made these comments on March 5, 2007 to the Budget Committee of the Upper House, and repeated them on more than one occasion. For Abe and the revisionists, see Hayashi Hirofumi, "Disputes in Japan over the Japanese Military 'Comfort Women' System and Its Perception in History," *Annals of the American Academy of Political and Social Sciences* 617 (May 2008): 123–32; Hayashi Hirofumi, Tawara Yoshifumi and Watanabe Mina *"Muryama-Kōno danwa" minaoshi no sakugo: rekishi ninshiki to 'ianfu' mondai o megutte* (Kyoto: Kamogawa shuppan, 2013).

[20] "Details of Exchanges Between Japan and the Republic of Korea (ROK) regarding the Comfort Women Issue – From the Drafting of the Kōno Statement to the Asian Women's Fund – (Provisional Translation)," Cabinet Secretariat, June 20, 2014, accessed May 4, 2020, https://japan.kantei.go.jp/96_abe/documents/2014/140620.html.

"confused memories."[21] In 2016 UNESCO was considering a joint nomination by civic organizations in nine countries to include documents collectively entitled "Voices of the Comfort Women" in the International Memory of the World Register. Pressure from the Abe government resulted in a postponement of the matter in 2017, again with its allies claiming that the testimonies offered no persuasive proof of coercion.[22] But postponement or no, the ideologically driven government position did little to diminish the value of the women's testimonies in a world by now grown accustomed to relying on individual voices as a source of firsthand knowledge about the past.

Experts in several fields recognize the limits to the epistemological value of personal testimony, not least for accounts rendered more than a half-century later. Experience and neuroscience have both shown that human memory is malleable, that it changes over time, and that it is affected both by subsequent events and also by the stories that are socially available and acceptable at any given moment. Oral histories are influenced by interviewers and the questions they ask while testimonies of people with similar experiences, such as Holocaust survivors or comfort women, are also influenced by one another, as suggested by the so-called model comfort woman story that emerged in the early 1990s.[23] Many accounts followed a similar narrative arc, beginning with when the women were taken, by deception or force, at a young age, then recounting the hellish treatment in the brothels, ending with the physical and psychic aftermath of pain and shame after the war was over. While the details differed, the narrative template could sometimes flatten, omit, or embellish

---

[21] For a scholarly but typical example, Hata Ikuhiko, *Ianfu to senjo no sei* (Tokyo: Shinchōsha, 1999); expanded English version, Hata Ikuhiko *Comfort Women and Sex in the Battle Zone* (Lanham, MD: Hamilton Books, 2018).

[22] For example, a letter from Japanese scholars supporting the government's position: "Over 100 Scholars Oppose UNESCO Registration of 'Comfort Women' Documents," Japan Forward, accessed May 4, 2020, https://japan-forward.com/89-japanese-scholars-oppose-unesco-registration-of-comfort-women-documents/.

[23] Ueno Chizuko and Jordan Sand, "The Politics of Memory: Nation, Individual and Self," *History and Memory* 11, no. 2 (Fall/Winter 1999): 129–52 (here 143–44); Ueno Chizuko, Araragi Shinzō and Hirai Kazuko, eds., *Sensō to senbōryoku no hikakushi ni mukete* (Tokyo: Iwanami shoten, 2018). For "the paradigmatic story," see C. Sarah Soh, *The Comfort Women: Sexual Violence and Postcolonial Memory in Korea and Japan* (Chicago: University of Chicago, 2008), 46–51.

things, just as time, temperament, and trauma affected individual memories of their personal pasts. Even so, there could never be a single comfort women story. For whether read separately or taken as a whole, the diversity of experience among the comfort women came through well and true. To be sure, scholars continued to argue about the relative evidentiary weight of testimony and written sources, exemplified by the contrasting views of Yoshimi Yoshiaki and Ueno Chizuko, both standing in opposition to the nationalistic revisionists.[24] Despite the alleged difference between Yoshimi's insistence on the historian's normal practices of verification of the facts, whether in documents or testimonies, and Ueno's poststructuralist accommodation of multiple truths and subjective agency in the stories told by the comfort women, in the end the two scholars and activists shared rather similar views. In fact, it was not the historian Yoshimi but the right-wing nationalists who were document-obsessed, on the one hand—denying the military brothel system because of the lack of written proof—and dismissive of the comfort women's testimonies as "fabrications" because of inconsistencies and factual errors, on the other.[25]

And yet, it seems clear to almost everyone—except Japanese conservative nationalists—that the comfort women were telling stories they did not invent and relating experiences that were common enough to appear in testimonies across a broad swath of Asia and among radically diverse groups of women. It is also clear that the soldiers who used the comfort stations told of their experiences, too, both before and after the comfort women came forth to tell of theirs. It follows that insistence on the utter unreliability of testimony is untenable, precisely because the assemblage of witnesses produced what even Japanese courts called irrefutable knowledge of past injustice. This epistemological change—a change in accepted modern ways of historical knowing based not on new but on renewed respect for the evidence of testimony, came about largely through remembering the atrocities of the Second World War.

---

[24] Ueno Chizuko, "Kioku no seijigaku: kokumin, kojin, watashi," *Inpakushon* 103 (1997), 154–74.

[25] For example, one of the many tendentious articles distributed by the right-wing Society for the Dissemination of Historical Fact: Nishioka Tsutomu, "Behind the Comfort Women Controversy: How Lies Become Truth," accessed May 16 2020, http://www.sdh-fact.com/book-article/229/.

Rights: Changes in the Realm of Rights

After law and testimony, the third marked change in memory practices occurred in the realm of rights, where public memory came to be linked to social justice of a civic sort. In many cases, this link appeared early in claims for the rights of the unincluded. Because dominant national narratives of the war began as simple black-and-white stories with a putatively unified nation as the subject of the story, they naturally excluded the wartime experiences of many people. Over the postwar years, those who were not included in the main national narratives of the war worked to have their stories recognized in the commons of public memory. These memory activists, as I have long called them, were countless in number, reflecting wartime experience of every conceivable kind, including all points across the political spectrum. Their associations and their activism brought pressure "from below"—from outside the state—on behalf of their *rights of memory*, thus providing one of the main levers of change in the all-too-simple narratives of the war so long dominant in official and popular memory.[26]

What then are the rights of memory? Those excluded from the national story of the past, and often disadvantaged in the national society of the present—frequently but not always victims—typically sought a combination of four demands: recognition, which included both knowledge and acknowledgment of their experience; compensation, as a measure of redress for injury done to them; education, in order to transmit that knowledge to future generations; and public apology, as open expression of remorse for the injustices of the past. Monetary compensation was important but generally secondary—for how could money redeem such incalculable loss?—while *knowledge and acknowledgment* appeared as the main demand. And the source of that acknowledgment had to be public, official, with the authority of history behind it, which nearly always meant the state. It had also to be visible, in the form of public memorials, commemorative anniversaries, parliamentary resolutions, and the like. Recognition had to include an educational component, which so many memorials came to do, whether of the Holocaust or African-American slavery. The proliferation of "memorial museums" in the late twentieth

---

[26] Carol Gluck, "Operations of Memory: 'Comfort Women' and the World," in *Ruptured Histories: War, Memory, and the Post-Cold War in Asia*, eds. Sheila Miyoshi Jaeger and Rana Mitter (Cambridge MA: Harvard University Press, 2007), 47–77.

century reflected this injunction, which was a combination of "never forget" and "never again." Similar patterns appeared in nearly every society, not only in regard to war memory but to many forms of past grievances, from state violence in Latin America to racial apartheid in South Africa. And these rights of memory were understood and demanded, not in judicial or emotional terms, but as *civil rights* or *social rights*—claims made by citizens on the state and society on the basis of human rights.

Such were the claims made in the testimonies of the former comfort women. They spoke of justice: "I want to see justice done before I die," was a common plaint.[27] By justice they meant recognition of the truth of their experience, which in turn was linked to apology and compensation, both from the Japanese government. This demand was one reason why some former comfort women rejected the so-called atonement payments from the Asian Women's Fund established in Japan in 1995 at the time of the fiftieth anniversary of the end of the war, under a government that had accepted the Kōno statement of two years earlier.[28] Those who did not accept the payments rejected them because the compensation came from a non-governmental organization, not from the state. Twenty years later in December 2015 an agreement between Japan and South Korea created another fund for compensation, this time from the Japanese government, but without consulting the dwindling number of surviving former comfort women and without a direct apology from Prime Minister Abe. One survivor, age eighty-eight, repeated a point she had made before: "We are not craving for money ... what we demand is that Japan make official reparations for the crime it has committed."[29]

The demand for education both centered on and in a number of instances also transcended gendered memory. The comfort women represented systematic sexual violence against women, which included not only

---

[27] For example, the memoir of the first Filipina *Lola* (as the former comfort women are called in the Philippines) to tell her story in public: Rosa Marie Henson, *Comfort Women: Slave of Destiny* (Manila: Philippine Center for Investigative Journalism, 1996), 152.

[28] See http://www.awf.or.jp/ for the official Japanese view of the fund; for a critique, Nishino Rumiko, Kim Puja and Onozawa Akane, eds. *'Ianfu' basshingu o koete; 'Kōno danwa' to Nihon no sekinin* (Tokyo: Ōtsuki shoten, 2013), in English, *The Japanese State's Assault on Historical Truth* (London: Routledge, 2018); for a defense, Ōnuma Yasuaki, Shimomura Mitsuko, Wada Haruki, *'Ianfu' mondai to Ajia josei kikin* (Tokyo: Tōshindō, 1998).

[29] Lee Yong-soo, quoted in Choe Sang-Hun, "Japan and South Korea Settle Dispute Over Wartime 'Comfort Women'," *New York Times*, December 28, 2015, https://www.nytimes.com/2015/12/29/world/asia/comfort-women-south-korea-japan.html.

military brothels but rape, mutilation, and murder of the sort that occurred during massacres in Nanjing and elsewhere as well as the wider range of such ongoing practices as sexual trafficking. At the same time many demands for redress avoided the conventional (male) language of the violation of female dignity, honor, or in South Korea, even "chastity." Instead, the grievances were presented as a violation of *human rights*—not women's rights, but the human rights of women.[30] In this way the activists and the survivors sought to move the comfort women from shame to rights, from injury to redress, from invisibility to citizenship. And they did so via the rights of memory.

A related idea appeared in the "Right to the Truth" articulated by the United Nations in 2006, an idea that had a long postwar history, sharpened by the demand of relatives to know the truth about the disappearances of their family members in Latin America in the 1970s, and heightened since the 1990s by war, genocide, and other violations of human rights. The UN described the right to the "full and complete truth" about gross human rights violations as "an inalienable and autonomous right, linked to the duty and obligation of the State to protect and guarantee human rights."[31] Moreover, since the 1990s it had become common to insist on "the universality, indivisibility, interdependence, and interrelatedness of civil, political, economic, social and cultural rights."[32] According to this strong, if aspirational, assertion, the right to the truth was now a right that tied doing justice to the past to civic and human rights in the present: in short, the rights of memory.

---

[30] This formulation became the rallying cry at the World Conference on Human Rights in Vienna in 1993, informed the Beijing Declaration and Platform for Action at the Beijing Conference on Women in 1995, and has remained on the UN agenda ever since. See "Women's Rights are Human Right," The Office of the High Commissioner for Human Rights, accessed May 16, 2020, https://www.ohchr.org/Documents/Events/WHRD/WomenRightsAreHR.pdf.

[31] "Promotion and Protection of Human Rights: Study on the Right to the Truth - Report of the Office of the United Nations High Commissioner for Human Rights," Commission on Human Rights, accessed May 16, 2020, https://documents-dds-ny.un.org/doc/UNDOC/GEN/G06/106/56/PDF/G0610656.pdf?OpenElement.

[32] For example, "Right to the Truth 10 October 2012," UN Human Rights Council Resolution, accessed May 16, 2020, http://www.ohchr.org/EN/Issues/Truth/Documents/A_HRC_21_7.pdf. The phrase dates at least from the World Conference on Human Rights, Vienna, 1993.

Politics: Change in Practices of Public Memory

Law, testimony, rights, and now politics—the politics of memory, too, changed over the course of the decades after 1945. In domestic terms, the war was of course fought by nations in the name of nations so that war memory everywhere enshrined national ideologies of identity, pride, and sacrifice. War memory was political from the first, and subsequent shifts in domestic politics affected public memory, especially that of the institutional or official sort.

China, for example, did not much engage in large-scale national commemoration of the Second World War during the Maoist era, especially in comparison with the anniversaries of the 1949 Revolution.[33] The government view of the war focused on Chinese Communist heroism in the Anti-Japanese War of Resistance, as World War II is known in China, and took the stance that it was not the Japanese people but their militarist leaders who had been responsible for the war. Then, in the 1980s, in the context of consolidating political power after the death of Mao, shifting from class struggle to economic growth, and making overtures to Taiwan, "a new remembering" of the war began to take hold in official discourse.[34] The government turned to patriotic education, which presented the war with an emphasis on Japanese atrocities and Chinese victimhood. 1985, the fortieth anniversary of the end of the war, saw a national ramp-up in commemoration, including the opening of the Nanjing Massacre Memorial Hall, and in a nod to Taiwan, a growing recognition of the Nationalists' contributions to the "All-nation War of Resistance." After the democracy protests in Tiananmen Square in 1989, for reasons of strengthening state power, the government intensified patriotic education, again featuring Japanese atrocities and Chinese suffering. The intensification continued under Xi Jinping, notably around the seventieth anniversary of the end of the war in 2015. Two of three new national holidays established in 2014 commemorated the war, one on December 13 for the Nanjing Massacre, the other on September 3, for the signing of Japan's surrender. The government designated nearly 200 national memorial sites related to the war; and on September 3, 2015, Xi Jinping presided over the largest military

---

[33] For official war memory before 1982 and the gap between it and popular views, see Chan Yang, *World War Two Legacies in East Asia: China Remembers the War I* (London: Routledge, 2017).

[34] For this phrase, see Arthur Waldron, "China's New Remembering of World War II: The Case of Zhang Zizhong," *Modern Asian Studies* 30, no. 4 (1996): 945–78.

parade ever held in Beijing. "History Cannot Be Distorted," stated the title of one of Xi's anniversary speeches, but it could clearly be instrumentalized for the sake of strengthening a political regime.

Vladimir Putin followed a similar pattern in Russia. He expanded the patriotic commemorations of Victory Day (May 9), especially on the sixtieth and seventieth anniversaries in 2005 and 2015. With the annexation of Crimea in 2014, when opposing sides were hurling epithets of "Nazis" and "fascists" at one another, Putin signed a new law making it a criminal offense to "spread intentionally false information about the Soviet Union's activities during World War II" and "to publicly desecrate symbols of Russia's military glory."[35] The Great Patriotic War, as it is known, had long been the centerpiece of Soviet and Russian national memory, and Putin, like nationalist leaders elsewhere, was deploying the politics of the past in the name of power in the present.

In Japan, the politics of war memory played out in official terrain largely through the Liberal Democratic Party (LDP), whose members over the years took positions that angered South Koreans, Chinese, and others, including many Japanese. Such incidents included prime ministers visiting Yasukuni, the shrine of the war dead; cabinet members denying the realities of the Nanjing Massacre; the Abe government refusing to recognize coercion of the comfort women; and the like. The memory politics of the LDP was partly a product of nationalist true believers, partly a position addressed to its right-wing supporters, and partly a refusal to acknowledge the way the winds of transnational memory were blowing. Notably, when the LDP fell in 1993 after nearly four decades in power, the first non-LDP prime ministers followed a different line, even traveling on what were nicknamed "apology tours" to Asian countries. When the LDP lost power again in 2009, the new prime minister immediately decided not to visit Yasukuni, suggesting that not every Japanese politician would work from the same playbook. Indeed, not every LDP leader did either. Miyazawa Kiichi, the prime minister when the Korean former comfort women filed their suit against the Japanese government in December 1991, expressed his "sincerest apology" in Seoul as early as January 1992. And Kōno Yōhei, who acknowledged military involvement in the comfort stations and the presence of coercion in his 1993 statement, was at the time the Chief Cabinet Secretary of an LDP government. But it was a different politician

---

[35] Ivan Kurilla, "The Implications of Russia's Law against the 'Rehabilitation of Nazism'," *PONARS Eurasia Policy Memo*, no. 331 (August 2014): 1–5.

and a different political context when the LDP returned to power in a coalition government in December 2012. Combining his own nationalistic beliefs with an electoral appeal to the conservative base of the party, Abe Shinzō made the comfort women a campaign issue, even pledging if elected to revise the Kōno Statement, twenty years after it was issued. Such were the domestic politics of war memory.

Yet the more decisive memory effect occurred in the arena of geopolitics. For if war memory was always national, memory of a world war was also always international. The dominant national narratives of the war originated in a geopolitical context that helped to determine the shape they took. For Japan that context was the Allied (American) occupation, which oversaw the renaming of the conflict as the Pacific War, reducing it chronologically to 1941–45, Pearl Harbor to Hiroshima, that is, the war between Japan and the United States. As a consequence the China War—total war from 1937 to 1945—faded out of the main story, and with it the wartime experiences of the peoples of East and Southeast Asia. Many in Japan accepted this congenial version of the past, which was reinforced by postwar domestic peace and prosperity, and frozen into place by the US-Japanese alliance during the Cold War. Then in the 1980s, and dramatically after the end of the Cold War in 1989, Japan confronted a different world, one in which the rise of Asia was transforming the geopolitical context, and with it, the memory of the Second World War.

In this respect, East Asia had much in common with Eastern Europe, in that both regions experienced a surge of war memory in the 1990s, as the long-dominant narratives—the Japanese story of the Pacific War under the American Cold War imperium; the Eastern European memories subsumed in a story of anti-fascism under the aegis of the Soviet Union—broke apart in contentious national and international debate about the publicly unremembered parts of the wartime past. And so it was said that the geopolitical postwar era in East Asia and Eastern Europe truly began only after 1989. The contrast with Western Europe was stark, precisely because countries like France and Germany had been working at postwar reintegration and reconciliation since the late 1940s. For this reason the geopolitics of war memory during the seventieth-anniversary year of 2015 was particularly vexed between, for example, Poland or the Baltics and Russia just as it was between Japan and South Korea, while the commemorations in Western Europe and North America seemed almost sleepy and formulaic in comparison.

For Japan, confronting its wartime past after the end of the Cold War meant dealing with the China War, thirty-five years of colonial rule in Korea, and the range of Japanese wartime actions and atrocities across East and Southeast Asia and in the Pacific. During the 1990s Koreans, Chinese and others increased the pressure on Japan to acknowledge these officially unacknowledged pasts. In this geopolitical context, in January 1992, the former Korean comfort women and their supporters began their weekly Wednesday demonstrations in front of the Japanese embassy in Seoul. On the day of the thousandth demonstration in 2011, the now famous bronze statue of a seated comfort woman was erected on that site. The demonstrations continued for decades afterward, even as the number of survivors shrank and their age rose to an average close to ninety. By the late 1990s, Chinese and Korean leaders had raised Japan's "history problem" to a regional political issue.

The regional issue was internationalized further as Chinese- and Korean-American and Canadian activists expanded their efforts to communicate Japanese wartime actions to wider audiences and to press for official demands on Japan to remember the Nanjing Massacre, POWs, the comfort women, and so on. There followed in the mid-2000s a series of parliamentary and congressional resolutions in Canada, the Netherlands, the EU, the US and other places, calling on Japan to confront the dark sides of its wartime past. In January 2014, the US Congress even passed a law, however ineffectual, demanding that Japan do so. Statues and memorials to the comfort women were erected in Korean-American communities in New Jersey, California, and soon other places as well, supported not only by Asian-Americans but by students, feminists, and others.[36] Of course, like most memory activists, these groups had their own agendas, whether of ethnic identity, gender, or local politics. But the collective outcome of their respective concerns was to take the comfort women issue across national and regional borders, adding the diverse voices of transnational civil society to those of international organizations like the United Nations. By 2017, there were statues and memorials in Germany, China, Taiwan, Australia, with proposals for more. The strenuous efforts of the Japanese government to protest the statues had the opposite of their intended effect. Indeed, it seemed as if every time Japanese diplomats opposed a memorialization of the comfort women in one place, a new

---

[36] Thomas J. Ward and William D. Lay, *Park Statue Politics: World War II Comfort Women Memorials in the United States* (Bristol: E-International Relations, 2019).

statue was erected somewhere else. In fact, the comfort women had become universalized as what one scholar terms "global victims" whose "symbolic power" was by then out of Japanese or even Asian hands.[37]

Meanwhile in the regional context, in 2011 the South Korean Constitutional Court ruled that the failure of the Korean government to seek compensation for the comfort women was a constitutional violation of the basic human rights of the victims. This unexpected judicial ruling brought law into diplomatic politics, requiring the government to engage with the issue in a new way in its relations with Japan.[38] After the ruling, Korean officials pursued the issue before the UN Human Rights Council in Geneva and in New York. The United Nations, whose censure of the comfort women system dated back to the 1996 Coomaraswamy report on "military sex slavery in wartime," continued through the 2010s to call for Japan to confront the comfort women issue and settle its dispute with South Korea.[39] The Japanese government, for its part, continued to protest the UN reports and censure.[40] Like Japanese courts, the government argued on the basis of its long-held premise that part of the 1965 normalization of relations between the two countries included a settlement which had, in the words of the agreement, "completely and finally"

---

[37] The argument is based on Holocaust survivors and others, but the comfort women also fit the description. Carolyn J. Dean, *The Moral Witness: Trials and Testimony after Genocide* (Ithaca, NY: Cornell University Press, 2019), 21–25.

[38] The South Korean ruling contravened the doctrine of avoiding "political questions," a doctrine upheld in 2012 by the Philippines Supreme Court in a similar case brought by Filipino comfort women. Monica E. Eppinger, Karen Knop and Annelise Riles, "Diplomacy and Its Others: The Case of Comfort Women," *Scholarship Commons*, Saint Louis University School of Law (2014): 23–45. For some reasons that might account for the South Korean court's ruling, Hideki Okuzono, "South Korean Judiciary Shakes Japan-South Korea Relations," *International Circumstances in the Asia-Pacific Series*, Japan Digital Library (March 2016): 1–12 (here 4–5).

[39] "Compilation of Recommendations by the UN Human Rights Bodies on the 'Comfort Women' Issue," Japan/Alternative Report on the Issue of Japan's Military Sexual Slavery May 2014, accessed May 16, 2020, https://tbinternet.ohchr.org/Treaties/CCPR/Shared%20Documents/JPN/INT_CCPR_CSS_JPN_17435_E.pdf.

For a representative official Japanese response, see e.g., Okamura Yoshifumi, "Letter from Ambassador Extraordinary and Plenipotenitary for Human Rights Okamura to Chair Janina of the Committee on Enforced Disappearance," Ministry of Foreign Affairs of Japan, accessed May 16, 2020, https://www.mofa.go.jp/policy/postwar/page22e_000883.html.

[40] For a summary of Japanese official rebuttals, see "Japan's Efforts on the Issue of the Comfort Women," *Diplomatic Bluebook 2019*, Ministry of Foreign Affairs of Japan, accessed May 16, 2020, https://www.mofa.go.jp/policy/postwar/page22e_000883.html.

resolved all claims made by South Korea on Japan. Koreans who thought otherwise were bolstered in their views by the 2011 ruling of the Constitutional Court demanding that the government take action on behalf of the surviving former comfort women.

Calls for compensation and "victim-centered" resolution of the dispute were accompanied by an unrelenting emphasis on the need for a government apology. Indeed, the politics of apology that developed in the decades since World War II paralleled the influence of domestic political concerns and changing geopolitics on East Asian war memory. By the end of the twentieth century it had become common to expect states to apologize to their citizens for injustices like slavery and mistreatment of indigenous peoples on the one hand, and to apologize to other states for wrongs committed during wartime and colonial rule on the other. Hence, the demands by Poland and the Baltic states for apologies from Russia for the depredations of World War II, and hence the calls on Japan for apologies to the former comfort women. The phenomenon of state apologies, which did not exist in this form seventy-five years ago, was now widespread. We live, asserted one scholar in "a guilted age."[41] Whatever one thinks of such official expressions of remorse—sincere or not—the politics of apology had become accepted, expected international practice.

When it comes to war memory, international practice matters, and not only for strictly political reasons. I have argued that change in national narratives of war is often impelled *from below*—from memory activists in civil society—but such change also comes *from outside*, from international pressure. The pressure can be geopolitical, as in the case of the reintegration of West Germany into Cold-War Europe and the demands now placed on Japan from the "neighboring countries" in post-Cold-War East Asia. International opinion plays a similar, often independent role in challenging national memories, as it did in responding to the Nazi genocide of the Jews in the years following the war and as it does currently in viewing the comfort women system as a violation of the human rights of women. Just as Holocaust memory no longer belongs to Germany alone, so, too, do the comfort women now occupy a place in transnational memory. International forces, both geopolitical and ethical, are thus not likely to cease calling on the Japanese government to follow current political practices in acknowledging past injustices.

---

[41] Ashraf H.A. Rushdy, *A Guilted Age: Apologies for the Past* (Philadelphia: Temple University Press, 2015).

When the Japanese and South Korean foreign ministers signed the December 2015 agreement that set up the Reconciliation and Healing Foundation to compensate the surviving comfort women, they declared the resolution to be "final and irreversible." But the politics of memory knows no such historical finality, and it often proves reversible, too. In this case, it took no time at all to demonstrate the futility of such diplomatic wishful thinking. Indeed, it had been sabotaged at the moment of the agreement by the Japanese demand that the comfort woman statue be removed from its place in front of their embassy in Seoul, a demand met with vehement public opposition in South Korea. In a typical poll, three-quarters of the Korean respondents were against moving the statue, and an even larger number (84%) thought that Japanese government had not apologized to the former comfort women.[42] No matter how often Japanese officials pointed to the number of public apologies Japan had offered since the first one made by Prime Minister Miyazawa in 1992, critics in Korea, China, Europe, the US, and elsewhere continued to deem them insufficient. The new South Korean president, Moon Jae-in (elected in 2017) rejected the 2015 bilateral agreement, declaring that the issue would be solved "only when the world, including ourselves and Japan, deeply reflects on sexual violence against all women."[43] He made this speech on the first commemoration in 2018 of a newly established national day in memory of the comfort women on August 14, the date Korea was liberated from Japanese colonial rule in 1945. Thus, he appealed to world opinion on women's rights on an occasion clearly linked in the public mind to an emotional evocation of Japan's oppressive colonial and wartime rule.

This mixed appeal to transnational values and national emotions aptly mirrored the memory politics characteristic of the "age of apologies," which itself was an outcome of a "normative cascade" that occurred over the decades since World War II. Redress and apology to the victims of past injustice became an international norm that spread together with human rights discourse and made coming to terms with the past "a tool of international politics."[44] But it was always a tool wielded in the service of national politics as well. National pride polarized domestic opinion in

---

[42] *Jiji tsūshin nyuusu*, September 2, 2016.
[43] *Nikkei Asian Review*, August 15, 2018.
[44] Stephanie Wolfe, *The Politics of Reparations and Apologies* (New York: Springer, 2014), 167–70, 178.

South Korea and Japan, suggesting that the "apology drama" between the two countries would continue, at least as long as conservative LDP governments remained in power in Japan.[45] Yet the changes in the global practice of memory politics also suggested that at some point, for the sake of regional and international relations, the Japanese government—however afflicted with so-called apology fatigue—would again apologize to and for the comfort women. For such are the political norms in the age of apologies.

Responsibility: Changes in Accountability for the Past

The fifth change in the global memory culture since 1945 related to conceptions of responsibility. In the simplest terms, responsibility for World War II was initially assigned to demonic or militaristic leaders, then broadened to those implicated by their positions in "organizational guilt," later widened still further to "ordinary men" who were involved in the atrocities of war, until finally it came to include society at large, bystanders as well as collaborators. Immediately after the war, both in national narratives and the international war crimes tribunals, Hitler, Mussolini, Tōjō, and their fellow leaders were considered responsible for waging aggressive war, a war that led to crushing defeat for the three Axis powers. Frequently described as a "handful" of evil or misguided leaders who misled their people, such a small number of leaders could scarcely have by themselves waged a total war that engaged all parts of state and society. In postwar reckonings with the Holocaust, the circle of official responsibility was enlarged to include organizational functionaries, so-called desk perpetrators, bureaucratic figures like Eichmann who claimed of his role in genocide that he was just "following orders."[46] By the 1990s, the sweep of responsibility had broadened further to include "ordinary men," who committed acts of horror, whether police battalions in the Holocaust by bullets in Eastern Europe or conscript soldiers during the Nanjing

---

[45] For "apology drama," Hiro Saito, "The Cultural Pragmatics of Political Apology," *Cultural Sociology* 10, no. 4 (2016): 448–65.
[46] Eichmann at his 1961 trial: David Cesarani, *Eichmann: His Life and Crimes* (London: Heinemann, 2004), 237–323.

Massacre.⁴⁷ Whatever coercion of command they may have experienced, they and many others, including civilians, could still be held accountable for their actions during the war.

By the end of the twentieth century the probing social histories of fascism, militarism, imperialism, and wartime occupation cast the political and moral net more widely still, implicating even more ordinary citizens, often called bystanders, whose accountability rested in their non-action, or acquiescence in the face of events they might have silently opposed, whether out of self-interest or reasonable fear of the consequences of speaking out. In short, total war now seemed to suggest total complicity. Such complicity was not the same as collective guilt, an earlier idea roundly rejected after the Second World War, but rather the responsibility of individuals in their respective civic contexts. This broadening of the range of responsibility usually derived less from the act of war itself than from moral atrocities committed in its name. The expansion of the concept of responsibility partly explained why wartime occupation and collaboration received increasing attention again after the turn of the century. In Vichy France, colonial Korea, Japanese-occupied East Indies, and many other places, the question became what made civilians behave as they did, and in what way were they to be held responsible for actions that at the time seemed sensible, useful, and even necessary.

While the idea of individual, rather than collective, responsibility gained ever greater prominence, a related question arose as to the extent of transgenerational responsibility. Across how many generations—to take the most common example—were young Germans expected to "inherit" the responsibility for the actions of their Nazi forebears. In 2004, when for the first time a German chancellor appeared with the French president at the commemoration of the Normandy landings, Chancellor Schröder suggested that "With regard to future generations, we should speak less about culpability and much more about responsibility."⁴⁸ The *responsibility* of citizens to recognize such unsavory parts of their nation's past as slavery and wartime atrocities is clearly different from *guilt* for having participated in them. Responsibility carries over to subsequent generations but guilt does not. The notion of "postwar responsibility" (*sengo sekinin*) used by

---

⁴⁷ The phrase made famous by Christopher R. Browning in his *Ordinary Men: Reserve Police Battalion 101 and the Final Solution in Poland* (New York: HarperCollins, 1992).
⁴⁸ *Le Monde*, June 5, 2004.

some in Japan expressed a similar thought, if not so directly.[49] Transgenerational responsibility also relates to transgenerational justice of the sort claimed as a right to the truth for the grandchildren of the Disappeared in Latin America and in the current claims for compensation by families and descendants for injustices done to past generations during the war. One might claim that some of the young activists across the globe who took up the cause of the comfort women were themselves bearing transgenerational responsibility for violations of the human rights of women long before they or even their parents were born.

Public opinion polls on war memory conducted since the 1990s suggested that the Japanese public understood their transgenerational relation to the past. In 2009, 49% thought Japan should apologize to the comfort women, 58% of those in their thirties and forties. In 2013, 75% disapproved of Osaka Mayor Hashimoto's remark that the comfort women were necessary to "offer rest" for the soldiers. In 2014, a poll found that 64% of university students surveyed thought the Japanese government should apologize to and compensate the victims. In a July 2015 poll, in which only 6% of respondents had experienced the war, 49% considered the war a "war of aggression" and 67% thought that Prime Minister Abe should apologize for colonial rule and aggression before and after the war in his seventieth-anniversary speech in August.[50] Important here were "communities of memory" that expressed a social consensus of the sort that came to exist about slavery in most places, and would perhaps one day come to exist about sex slavery, too.[51] And should that happen, it would be due in part to the former comfort women and their advocates around the world.

The stress on individual civic responsibility and the responsibility of states to their citizens and indeed to other states and *their* citizens found an echo in the thinking that underlay the United Nations commitment to R2P: Responsibility to Protect. Endorsed by the member states in 2005, the doctrine was described as a new international security and human rights norm to address the international community's failure to prevent and stop genocides, war crimes, ethnic cleansing, and crimes against

---

[49] For example, Ōnuma Yasuaki, *Tōkyō saiban, sensō sekinin, sengo sekinin* (Tokyo: Toshindō, 2007); Takahashi Tetsuya, *Sengo sekininron* (Tokyo: Kōdansha, 1999).

[50] *Chosun ilbo*, October 20, 2009; *Asahi shinbun*, May 20, 2013; *Kyōdō tsūshin*, September 27, 2014; *Kyodo News* July 21, 2015.

[51] W. James Booth, *Communities of Memory: On Witness, Identity, and Justice* (Ithaca: Cornell University Press, 2006).

humanity. A response in part to Rwanda and Srebrenica, it enjoined the world to "never forget the victims of atrocities and crimes." To exercise "collective responsibility" was to commit to work together to prevent them.[52] However unreachable an ideal, it was born of the changes in ideas of historical responsibility that had occurred over the course of the twentieth century.

GLOBAL MEMORY CULTURE IN AN AGE OF RISING NATIONALISMS

The changes in law, testimony, rights, politics, and responsibility together constitute what I have been calling a *global memory culture*. Although based in part on precedents, its current form gradually emerged in the decades after 1945, to a considerable extent through debates and developments in the changing public memories of World War II. By the turn of the twenty-first century the global memory culture possessed its own norms and expectations, processes, and practices. States and societies were now expected to practice a politics of memory that included knowledge and acknowledgment of past actions; apologies and compensation to victims of injustice; education and memorialization to transmit their memory to future generations; and a general, collective, public, and official confrontation with the dark as well as the bright parts of a nation's past. The Holocaust figured in many of the changes outlined here, from trials to notions of responsibility, transforming the Holocaust into a *traveling trope*: a transnational and global referent for genocide. In the years after 1991, the comfort women, too, became a traveling trope: a transnational and global referent for the violation of the human rights of women. If, as Ueno Chizuko said of the comfort women in 1995, it had taken fifty years to change "the shame of women" into "the crime of men," it was also true that by the end of the 1990s people in Japan, Asia, and around the world came to know about the comfort women and what they represented.[53]

---

[52] "United Nations Office on Genocide Prevention and the Responsibility to Protect," accessed May 16, 2020, https://www.un.org/en/genocideprevention/about-responsibility-to-protect.shtml; "Never forget the victims of Atrocities, Urges Secretary-General as He Opens Special General Assembly Session on Implementing Responsibility to Protect," accessed May 16, 2020, https://www.un.org/press/en/2009/ga10845.doc.htm.

[53] Ueno Chizuko, "Kioku no seijigaku: kokumin, kojin, watashi," 154.

Their experience was written into international law in the 1998 statute of the International Criminal Court, which made wartime rape a crime against humanity, and references to the comfort women frequently appeared in the ongoing UN campaigns for the elimination of gender-based violence and the Elimination of Discrimination Against Women. UN reports from the mid-1990s used the term sex slavery for the comfort women system, a term vociferously opposed by the Japanese government and other conservatives but one that became established as part of a wider international discourse on trafficking, sexual violence, and rape. When it came to apology and compensation, speakers in UN deliberations often expressed the position held by South Korean officials and transnational civil society activists alike that human rights violations would not be settled "until the victims received satisfaction."[54] This victim-centered understanding of past (and present) injustices was itself a product of the global memory culture. In this instance it meant that the demands of the surviving former comfort women had to be satisfied; the issue could not be settled by the state without their participation—a criticism leveled at the "final and irreversible" 2015 agreement between Japan and South Korea. In sum, at the same time that the comfort women remained a flammable topic in the national and regional politics of memory in East Asia, they had also become a global referent in the international campaign for human rights. And having become part of transnational memory, transnational norms now placed pressure on the same Japanese official memory whose recalcitrance accelerated the international movement to recognize the comfort women in the first place.

Nationalism was surely the main obstacle to official Japanese recognition of the comfort women system and other malign parts of the wartime past. The resurgent nationalisms that afflicted so much of the post-Cold War world each wielded history as an instrument of national pride and patriotism at home and a geopolitical cudgel in regional relations abroad. In this regard, China, South Korea, and Japan exemplified a globally widespread revisiting—and revising—of national history to serve present political power. Nationalism suffused South Korean views on the comfort women to the point that it could seem that only a single narrative would

---

[54] For a typical example of UN claims and Japanese responses: "Committee on the Elimination of Discrimination Against Women Examines Reports of Japan," The Office of the High Commissioner for Human Rights, accessed May 16, 2020, https://www.ohchr.org/EN/NewsEvents/Pages/DisplayNews.aspx?NewsID=17052&LangID=E.

be permitted, not only in the court of public opinion, but in law courts as well. The South Korean scholar who described voluntary as well as coerced sexual service and wrote about the role of Korean recruiters of young girls in her study of the comfort women lost a 2015 lawsuit against her for defaming the honor of the victims and causing them mental stress. Her narrative of willing Korean participation in the comfort women system violated Korea's preferred national story of coercion and forced labor by Japan as the oppressive colonial and wartime power.[55] The Japanese government's response was just as predictably nationalistic, praising the book for affirming its stance that the comfort women were either prostitutes or sold by their families and were therefore not coerced. At issue were less the facts than the two national narratives, with each side trying to prevent the other from besmirching the nation's honor, in the process drawing Korea and Japan further away from the "reconciliation" that the author claimed was her goal in writing the book.[56]

The patterns of nationalistic memory politics differed from place to place, but in East Asia the most serious consequence of the recent contention might well turn out to be the attitudes of young people in each country. Although polls showed that they often knew little of the factual history of the war, new generations of so-called angry youth in China learned to hate the Japanese for wartime atrocities and national humiliation, and younger South Koreans responded to the escalation of the "history problem," which banked the fires of postcolonial hostility. Numbers of young Japanese responded with anger at the constant harping on Japan's shortcomings. The Internet harbored a vast swamp of regional hate speech, expressed in one's own language and directed to like-minded fellow Chinese, Korean, or Japanese youth. Far from being age- or even decades-old, this "hate nationalism," as I call it, surged after the turn of the century. And unlike the Abe regime, whose political power was finite, hostility learned in one's youth could last a lifetime.

The comfort women and other historical issues certainly affected attitudes toward relations between Japan and South Korea. Hate nationalism

---

[55] Pak Yu-ha, *Teikoku no ianfu: shokuminchi shihai to kioku no tatakai* (Tokyo: Asahi shinbun shuppan, 2014), the Japanese version by the author of the original, *Cheguk ŭi wianbu*, first published in Korean in 2013, reprinted in 2018, the versions differing somewhat one from the other. After appeals and support from in and outside South Korea, she lost the civil suit against her in the Seoul High Court in 2017.

[56] Pak's previous book was *Wakai no tame ni: kyōkasho, ianfu, Yasukuni, Tokutō* [Toward reconciliation: textbooks, comfort women, Yasukuni, Dokdo] (Tokyo: Heibonsha, 2006).

notwithstanding, polls in 2019 showed that young people had more favorable impressions of the other country than the general population, although larger percentages of Japanese youth had a "bad impression" of Korea than vice versa. Half the Japanese with a negative impression of Korea gave the "continued criticism of history issues" as the reason for their opinion. The top reason for Koreans' negative impression of Japan, given by three quarters of those polled, was that Japan had not "properly reflected on its history of invading South Korea." And both sides gave "resolving historical disputes (comfort women/forced labor)" as the most important issue necessary to improve bilateral relations.[57] Prospects for resolution seemed less than rosy in another 2019 poll, in which 87% of South Koreans wanted further apologies from Japan, while 80% of Japanese believed that additional apologies were unnecessary.[58] These figures reversed in the past and they could well reverse again, but they clearly demonstrated the volatility that nationalistic uses of the past could arouse within nations and between them.

But because the comfort women, like the Holocaust, transcended local and regional borders to become part of transnational memory, the issue was no longer confined to contention between Japan and other Asian countries. And because the norms of the global memory culture required official acknowledgment, apology, and compensation, it was unlikely that future Japanese governments would forever choose to evade living up to those norms. Yet the point of greater significance might well be the role played by the comfort women and their supporters in helping to bring the violation of the human rights of women to sufficient global visibility that people and institutions sought to do something to prevent such violations from continuing. One critical factor was the civil courage of the former comfort women—including the poor and powerless, some illiterate, all elderly, from different countries across Asia—in coming forth to tell their stories and bring their experiences, terrible as they were, to the attention of the world. A second critical factor was the global memory culture brought about by the changes in legal, social, political, and moral understanding of the rights of women, sexual violence, and of civic

---

[57] "The 7th Japan-South Korea Joint Public Opinion Poll, Analysis Report on Comparative Data 2019," The Genron NPO, accessed May 16, 2020, http://www.genron-npo.net/en/opinion_polls/archives/5489.html.

[58] "Poll: Japan, ROK see ties worsening," *The Japan News*, June 11, 2019, http://the-japan-news.com/news/article/0005803183.

responsibilities in times of war and peace. The norms and practices of the global memory culture combined with the spirit of these women to produce what might have seemed an unlikely scenario—maltreated women against a maltreating world—not only possible but successful in effecting change.

What the world owes the comfort women then is a debt both to the past, in the form of a more responsible public memory, and to the future, in the effort to prevent similar injustice in our own time.

Open Access This chapter is licensed under the terms of the Creative Commons Attribution 4.0 International License (http://creativecommons.org/licenses/by/4.0/), which permits use, sharing, adaptation, distribution and reproduction in any medium or format, as long as you give appropriate credit to the original author(s) and the source, provide a link to the Creative Commons licence and indicate if changes were made.

The images or other third party material in this chapter are included in the chapter's Creative Commons licence, unless indicated otherwise in a credit line to the material. If material is not included in the chapter's Creative Commons licence and your intended use is not permitted by statutory regulation or exceeds the permitted use, you will need to obtain permission directly from the copyright holder.

CHAPTER 5

Eddies and Entanglements: Africa and the Global Mnemoscape

Lauren van Der Rede and Aidan Erasmus

Fig. 5.1 The Ethiopian Red Terror Martyrs Memorial Museum in Addis Ababa, showing a replica of the blood-filled bottle used by Mengistu to signal the start of the Red Terror, the faces of 755 individuals on the Derg "wanted list" and (1977) (reflected in the vitrine) the faces of the disappeared who are still missing (Lauren van der Rede)

Abstract Van Der Rede and Erasmus provocatively characterize Africa as a "disobedient object" of memory studies, posing a series of radical challenges to the terms and methods of the field. In empirical terms, they point out how two specific cases, the Red Terror in Ethiopia and States of Emergency during Apartheid in South Africa, inflect our Europe-centered models of trauma and memory. Beyond this, positing Africa "not as a cartographic and geological location but as a concept and methodology," van Der Rede and Erasmus challenge the liberal universalism implicit in the problematics of memory studies (and indeed in the notion of mnemonic solidarity) with an insistence on hearing/listening rather than speaking that draws on postcolonial theory and the new methods of sound studies.

Keywords Africa and the global mnemoscape • Ethiopian Red Terror • South Africa's states of emergency • Genocide • Ethiopia • South African apartheid

Resisting the Knot: Memories and Their Allegiances

The grains of Ethiopia and South Africa's histories grate differently, though the irony with which they are held within the context of the study of the past is uncanny—be it memory or historical studies. The first of these spaces was never formally colonized, was itself an empire and remains synonymous with a politics of resistance, but is also a site of atrocities which the international community calls terror and local law recognizes as genocide. The second, in the infancy of its democracy, remains swaddled by the legacy of colonialism. It is a site of the extreme violence that accompanied institutionalized and legislated racism which

---

L. van Der Rede (✉)
Department of English, Stellenbosch University, Cape Town, South Africa
e-mail: lvdr@sun.ac.za

A. Erasmus
Department of History, University of the Western Cape, Bellville, South Africa
e-mail: aerasmus@uwc.ac.za

saw multiple states of emergency and yet is revered for its constitutional progressiveness. What drops out between the Ethiopian Red Terror and apartheid South Africa's states of emergency is precisely that around which they are congealed, become knotted together and in place, as "then and there" from the "here and now." Said differently, it is the refusal to think seriously not only of the violence of colonialism but of colonialism as violence that produces a knot from which African examples of genocide and war cannot come undone. Consequently, it remains that judgments pertaining to the veracity and value of violence lived and lives lost remain skewed. What the spaces of Ethiopia and South Africa offer us is a moment in and through which to respond to the call for a mnemonic solidarity: a call for the democratization of the global mnemoscape. This call, which itself carries a charge that requires attention, asks not so much what the form or content of a global mnemoscape might look like but rather what its movement looks like, the churning of its subjects and the eddying of its temporalities. To read, hear, and respond to mnemonic solidarity as a call—in some sense, a summons—has at the outset a grounding assumption: that one has the potential and capacity to both *hear* and *listen* of and to the persons whose subjecthood is textured by the discursive punctures of the global mnemoscape. We understand these punctures to be those ruptures that perforate the desire for a discourse of memory that might encompass the world through a different kind of solidarity of the present that can express the past without fetishizing it. These punctures, we argue, must be attended to if we are to embark on the task of the democratization of the global mnemoscape, let alone constitute a solidarity around its many parts.

Thus, in these terms, a call for mnemonic solidarity should be read as marking both a desire for and a movement toward dismantling the territorializing effect of mnemonic discourses on colonialism, war, and genocide. The desire aforementioned is a response to the multitemporal and multispatial sear of colonialism, war and genocide as violence as politics, still unfolding histories, and divergent memories. Moreover, this desire is embedded in the call to think through these expressions of violence in a mode that democratizes, without flattening contextual specificity, the global mnemoscape. To set to work and realize a global mnemoscape would mean abiding by this beckoning, and allowing an entanglement of memory that would democratize rather than universalize mnemonic discourses. If we are to address certain disciplinary and methodological inheritances, such an entanglement is critical, and particularly useful insofar as it is a system of value that does not conform to an ordering of human suffering that must produce hierarchies as its structuring dynamic.

What follows will be an attempt to register how one might responsibly answer such a beckoning, from the vantage point of a non-geographically demarcated Africa, and its stakes in the wake of the formulation and deployment of the global mnemoscape and its own desire for solidarity. We will explore this position through an analysis of what we deem two mnemonically disobedient devices: Ethiopia's Red Terror as genocide, and the ambiguity of time and war encapsulated in apartheid South Africa's states of emergency. South Africa and Ethiopia are mnemonically disobedient objects insofar as they bear the marks of the knottiness of their relation to the past in the present. They disobey injunctions to be rendered as constellations of violent events, refuse historicism as a logic of the past, and evade a register that would reduce its subjects and objects to violence laid bare. As disobedient signifiers that operate as subjects within the mnemoscape, they demand coevalness, they resist, unsettle, and undermine the disciplinary functions of the discourses of genocide, war, and colonialism. For better or worse, they bear the marks of a difference that troubles—eddies—the regime of historicity that would read colonialism as an event.

ETHIOPIA: EDDYING GENOCIDE AND TERROR

Ethiopia is one space through which to respond to a call of mnemonic solidarity. Having ratified the *Convention on the Prevention and Punishment of the Crime of Genocide* (1948) in the year of its enactment, the country later also translated the definition of genocide into its Penal Code (1957), expanding thereon to provide protection for not only racial, ethnic, national, and religious groups, but also political groups. It is as a result of this elaboration that after the dismantlement of the Derg regime in 1991, the Special Prosecutor for the local courts was able to charge persons responsible for the Ethiopian Red Terror (officially c. 1976–78) with the crime of genocide. By contrast, in the chambers of the International Criminal Court (ICC), perpetrators of the Red Terror could only be charged with War Crimes, as a recent case has shown.[1]

---

[1] "Ethiopia: 'Red Terror' war crimes trial begins at The Hague," *BBC*, October 30, 2017, https://www.bbc.com/news/world-africa-41802232.

In the years prior to, but also through and beyond, the Revolution of 1974, Ethiopia was a land of contradiction, stratified above all else by class divisions. The capital was home to well over a million Ethiopians, the vast majority of whom constituted the working middle and lower classes, who depended in many ways on the peasant class of Ethiopia for the agricultural supplies of everyday life. However, as a result of the famine(s) which ravaged rural Ethiopia in the early 1970s this chain of supply and demand was broken, and the plight of the rural in many ways thus became the plight of the urban. It was this permeation of urban and rural/upper and lower classes, and the cruel irony of the "Hidden Famine" of 1973 coinciding with the extravagance of Emperor Haile Selassie that ignited the Marxist-Socialist Revolution, led by parties of student movements and the intelligentsia, and consolidated by the military.

Following the deposition and later the murder of Emperor Haile Selassie in 1974 the Derg, a nominally Marxist faction which had splintered away from the rest of the military, took power and ruled Ethiopia until 1991, not through democratic redress but through fear. The Red Terror is generally associated with the years 1977–78, but it is important to note that the military junta's violence, indeed its brutality, did not spontaneously begin in 1977, or abruptly end in 1978; nor does it necessarily operate along these lines as memory. Rather the violence which reached a peak during those years, and many thereafter, had been creeping, slow to become visible but encroaching evermore on the peoples of Ethiopia. Some Ethiopians may have/still remember the brutality of the war with Italy, and its brief occupation in the 1930s, as well as the devastating and drawn-out conflict with Eritrea over its independence. Thus, the acts committed by the Derg as well as those under its command and civilian allies were made practice well before the revolution. Rather, through the terror the Derg returned the brutality perpetrated against Ethiopians in the name of Italian colonization, and against Eritreans who struggled for independence from Ethiopia since 1961, on Ethiopia itself. In this way the Derg did, much as Aimé Césaire argues the Nazis did to Europe, return the barbarity of colonialism and empire to Ethiopia.[2]

The Derg began a campaign of repression banning any opposition parties and inaugurating military rule, thus disavowing the desire for democratization. Moreover, it subjected its opponents to acts of cruelty which

---

[2] Aimé Césaire, *Discourse on Colonialism*, trans. J. Pinkham (New York: Monthly Review Press, 2000).

are considered gross human rights violations and crimes against humanity, including: killing, torture, abduction, and disappearance. However, the Derg also banned any "anti-revolutionary" literature, which is to say texts which attempted to activate resistance against the military regime, including "ABYOT," "Struggle,"[3] and others, going so far as to destroy the machinery of print. These acts of violence are not unique to the Derg and are familiar to presumably most persons in any part of the world today as expressions of particular kinds of logic. For example, killing, torture, disappearance are included as constitutive acts in the definition of genocide provided in international law by the United Nations (UN) Convention on the Prevention and Punishment of the Crime of Genocide (1948)[4] and the Rome Statute of the International Criminal Court (ICC) (1998).

Rather, as mentioned previously, what sets genocide aside from other forms of extreme and systemic violence is its *mens rea*: "... intent to destroy...." Terror's *mens rea*, however, may be understood as the desire to coerce another group into subjugation by holding them hostage through fear. As Igor Primoratz explains, the logic of terror is such that it works to intimidate "innocent" people "into a course of action that they would otherwise not take" through "the deliberate use of violence, or the threat of its use."[5] In this sense, terror has two targets. The first is the direct target of an attack, subjected to those acts which constitute the manifest, blatant violence of terror. This target is the person who is presumed to be an immediate threat to the regime and is subjected to forced disappearance and kidnapping, torture, and killing, and so on. Through rumor and the displaying of the deceased in the streets of the capital and its surrounds the Derg made that direct violence spectacular at the same time as it was clandestine. And when bodies were dumped in the city streets, this spectacular violence also became a part of the quotidian, as communities were directly policed through the clustering of every approximately five homes in a neighborhood (kebeles) administered by civil servants of the regime (kebele officers).

On the one hand, killing, abduction, disappearance, and torture served to illuminate the person identified as a threat to the regime. What is

---

[3] ABYOT was an independent, resistance pamphlet printed in both Amharic and English circulating as a mode of critiquing the Derg; while its English counterpart "Struggle" was a pamphlet published by the University Students' Union of Addis Ababa.

[4] Hereafter simply referred to as the Genocide Convention.

[5] Igor Primoratz, "What is Terrorism?" in *Terrorism: The Philosophical Issues*, ed. Igor Primoratz (New York: Palgrave Macmillan, 2004), 15–27.

significant to note here is that the identification of a person as an enemy of the Derg—and as such by extension the state—was not self-identification; the individual him/her/themselves did not necessarily identify as oppositional to the state, unless he/she/they were in fact a member of politically oppositional groups such as the Ethiopian People's Revolutionary Party (EPRP) and Meison. Rather, he/she/they needed only to be named, suspected and as such marked as an opponent to the regime in order for said person to be considered "anti-revolutionary," "terrorist," "anti-Ethiopia," and therefore necessary to eliminate. The condition for this elimination of an opponent, this first constellation of techniques of terror, is premised on conspiracy and suspicion, whereby the accused is presumed guilty until proven innocent.

The true brutality of the Derg's rule is that it rendered spectacular violence quotidian, and in so doing assaulted its second, indirect target—the civilians who survive to bear witness, and whose witnessing in turn produced the fear through which the Derg held hostage the population and simultaneously subjugated the people. This is the primary object of terror: The direct victim who is subjected to killing, torture, and so on is conscripted as a mechanism through which to activate the fear that will take hostage and subjugate those who remain. It is the indirect victim, left to live with the constant threat of being made a direct victim, who is of primary importance. In this sense the violence directly enacted on a single person is displaced onto a group of people. The dumping of victims' bodies in the streets of Addis Ababa is one of the techniques through which this is achieved, registering as public display the culmination of the cruelty of the Derg. It is a warning that inspires foreboding that is affirmed when messages are left on the body that read "I am an enemy of the people. Mother, don't weep for me, I deserved to die."[6] In some instances, these notes explaining murder as deserved punishment for (being suspected of) opposing the Derg are placed on the person before they are in fact executed—as an artwork in the Red Terror Martyrs Memorial Museum (RTMMM) in Addis Ababa suggests. In this artwork a row of people is depicted against a red, unevenly shaded backdrop; the first from the left appears to be a priest, then a woman, four men, a woman in front of whom stands a boy child, a woman in hijab, and finally another man. Of this scale of individuals, all of whom have their hands out of view (thus

---

[6] Maaza Mengiste, *Beneath the Lion's Gaze: A Novel* (New York: WW Norton & Company, 2010), 240.

presumably bound), and all are met with shadowed silhouettes shaped quite like a Kalashnikov.

What is at stake in the difference produced by the labeling of some of the soon-to-be-shot is that not all of the victims of the Derg and particularly the Red Terror were necessarily themselves members of political opposition or even identified as such. Some victims were subjected to this kind of violence purely on the grounds of being associated with someone who was presumed a threat to the regime. What this gestures toward is a feature of the figure of the terrorist which distinguishes it from the assassin or the revolutionary, for example. As Primoratz explains, this feature is the inability to distinguish between guilty and innocent, and in this context it is this inability that contributes along with the spectacular violence like that of the Derg, to the paranoia through which entire populations are held hostage through terror.

Techniques of terror are textured differently and include various mechanisms—activating gestures—that render it visible and audible to the primary target and in so doing produce witnesses and testimony, so as to activate fear. The public display of mutilated bodies, the refusal to return or reveal the location of the disappeared (living or not), and the letting live and release of victims of torture made knowable the extent of cruelty to which the Derg was willing to go. Terror through its mechanisms and techniques deploys fear's interpellative potential to subjugate.[7] Terror acts by rendering the spectacular quotidian. But the everydayness of the excessive violence in response to the anxiety of a regime is not mundane; despite its routineness and its imposed cohabitation the spectacular violence of the Derg's project of terror did not lose its charge. Rather it continued and continues in some ways to sear the lived experience of Ethiopians, as is clear from the growing exhibition in the Red Terror Martyrs Memorial Museum, in Addis Ababa.[8]

---

[7] On interpellation, see L. Althusser, "Ideology and Ideological State Apparatuses (*Notes towards an Investigation*)," in *Lenin and Philosophy and Other Essays*, trans. B. Brewster (New York: Monthly Review Press, 2001), 11–44.

[8] In addition to the sources listed in footnote 5, see Edward Kissi, "'Remembering Ethiopia's Red Terror: History of a Private Effort to Preserve a Public Memory," in *Documenting the Red Terror: Bearing Witness to Ethiopia's Lost Generation*, ed. Hirut Abebe-Jirut (Ottawa, Ethiopian Red Terror Documentation and Research Centre (ERTDRC), 2012), 9–24; Lauren van Der Rede, "Disappeared to Ethiopia's Bermuda: Tales by a Puppet," *Kronos* vol. 44 no. 1 (2018): 196–210, https://doi.org/10.17159/2309-9585/2018/v44a12; Deirdre McQuillan, "Ethiopia Still Haunted by Memory of Derg Genocidal

In the wake of the dismantling of the military regime in 1991, the Ethiopian state was tasked with addressing the atrocities committed as part of the terror sowed by the Derg, in the absence of any legal protections against the offense of "terrorism" or "terror." It is important to note that terrorism is a crime against international customary law, like genocide, but unlike genocide does not have a central guiding and accepted definition from which other forms of legislation, including local legislation, can take its cue.[9] Rather, terror is defined largely according to a state's own definitions (and needs), as South Africa did in 1967 and Ethiopia would do only in 2009. Accordingly, the members of the Derg who were tried during the Red Terror Trials were charged with the crime of and offenses relating to genocide, and not in fact terror. The prosecution relied on the definition of genocide provided by its Penal Code of 1957, which is an adaptation of the definition enshrined in the Genocide Convention (and later the Rome Statute). What enabled this is a distinguishing feature of the Ethiopian definition of genocide laid out in the Penal Code of 1957, namely that in addition to racial, ethnic, religious, or national groups, political groups are protected as well.

It was on these grounds that democratic Ethiopia took a retributive approach to justice and charged 27 members of the Derg, including "chairman" Mengistu Haile Mariam, with Crimes Against Humanity and Genocide, and not "Terrorism." This is significant because it gestures toward a misfire in the praxis of naming violence and attending to that violence. The irony of naming the atrocities committed in Ethiopia by the Derg *terror* but the charging perpetrators with *genocide* points a veiling of the eponymous quality of Ethiopia's Red Terror, which was named after the Red Terror perpetrated by the Bolsheviks in Russia approximately 60 years before. What is lost if we do not mark this irony is a turning to

---

Regime," *The Irish Times,* May 6, 2011, https://www.irishtimes.com/news/ethiopia-still-haunted-by-memory-of-derg-genocidal-regime-1.563626.

[9] Terrorism, as a legal concept, has proved slippery in so far as defining it as a crime of international law is concerned. However, since the 1960's there have been numerous sectoral counter-terrorism interventions. These include the *Convention on Offenses and Certain Other Acts Committed On Board Aircraft* (1963), the *Convention on the Physical Protection of Nuclear Material* (1979), the *International Convention for the Suppression of Terrorist Bombings* (1997), and the *International Convention for the Suppression of Acts of Nuclear Terrorism* (2005). See Ben Saul, "The Legal Response of the League of Nations to Terrorism," *Journal of International Criminal Justice* 4 (2006): 78–102; and Ben Saul, "Speaking of Terror: Criminalizing Incitement to Violence," *The University of New South Wales Law Journal (UNSW Law Journal)* 28 no. 3 (2005): 868–86.

Europe that is colored not by a desire to become a Westernized subject, but rather a desire to learn barbarity. The definition of genocide provided in the Ethiopian Penal Code of 1957 is more elaborate than the definition provided in the Genocide Convention and the Rome Statute. Under Article 281 of Title II of the Ethiopian Penal Code of 1957, Offenses against the Law of Nations, Chapter 1 (Fundamental Offenses) genocide is defined as follows:

> Genocide; Crimes against Humanity.
>
> Whosoever, with intent to destroy, in whole or in part, a national, ethnic, racial, religious, or political group, organizes, orders, or engages in, be it in time of war or in time of peace:
>
> (a) Killings, bodily harm or serious injury to the physical or mental health of members of the group, in any way whatsoever; or
> (b) Measures to prevent the propagation or continued survival of its members or their progeny; or
> (c) The compulsory movement or dispersion of peoples or children, or their placing under living conditions calculated to result in their death or disappearance, is punishable with rigorous imprisonment from five years to life, or, in cases of exceptional gravity, with death.

The disjuncture between this articulation of the crime of genocide and that of the Genocide Convention begins with its framing, or title, in which genocide and crimes against humanity are named alongside each other, as equally offensive and as such, of equal importance. However, the legislation above sands away the grains of difference between genocide and crimes against humanity. Although the constitutive acts are shared by the two offenses, the mental element of these crimes which produces them as different is negated. According to the Rome Statute genocide is committed with "intent to destroy, in whole or in part, a racial, ethnical, nation or religious group, as such" (Article 6); while crimes against humanity are violent acts committed "as part of a widespread or systematic attack directed against any civilian population, with knowledge of the attack" (Article 7). There are a number of reasons why the way in which the Ethiopian legislation expresses the *mens rea* shared between genocide and crimes against humanity is significant.

First, it marks the perpetrator of these crimes as a subject: "*who*soever," while neither the Genocide Convention nor the Rome Statute marks an activating agent in its definition of genocide, and in the case of the Rome

Statute, crimes against humanity. This invocation of the subject—indeed of the human—is significant because it marks that there are people on both sides of atrocity. Second, this guilty subject is not only a person who commits one of these acts him/her/theirself but also someone who orders or engages in it, thus preemptively undoing the defense that many Nazis used at Nuremberg during the Military Tribunals (1945–46). In doing so—in opening what it means to actively participate in atrocity—it also explodes the question of complicity. Thus, the third point of significance: that the Ethiopian Penal Code of 1957 was a response to the Holocaust, in that it translated genocide and crimes against humanity (an offense adopted in the Charter of the International Military Tribunal, or the Nuremberg Charter) into legislation as lessons from Nuremberg. Fourth, the legislation marks that both genocide and crimes against humanity can occur during times of war (between states) *and* peace.[10] This is important because it marks that interstate war is not violence's condition, but rather that there is the potential during times of peace for a different kind of war, in which the state reads as its enemy and takes as its target not another state and its agents, but its own people. This kind of war is what Raphael Lemkin in 1948 called genocide—what Ethiopians in the 1970s would call terror—and what South Africa for most of the second half of the twentieth century knew as apartheid.

Listening and Hearing: Of Modes

To achieve what a call for mnemonic solidarity whispers as its desired object requires reckoning with an Africa that sits beyond its geographic designation as place. This means that what is necessary is to register Africa as a concept for thinking the global mnemoscape as a site that is not situated, and what may be useful in this is a leaning toward modes of aurality—hearing and listening—as interpretive signposts to help us map the texture of the past in the present. The inclination to treat discourses on colonialism, war, and genocide as discrete is refused by such a gesture toward sound, and their differences are laid bare for analysis. Indeed, it is in the resonant movement of concepts such as genocide, war, and

---

[10] It is important to mark here that no Nazi was charged with the crime of genocide at Nuremberg, but that these persons were in fact charged with war crimes. Although the word genocide was used (once) during the Nuremberg proceedings, it only acquired the status of criminal offense in 1948.

colonialism that we might hear the unsettling of their groundedness, in either Europe or its Other. In the most salient ways genocide, war, and colonialism are marked by their intent: to destroy, to resolve, and, finally, to civilize. These intentions are further emboldened by a desire to improve the ways in which their intent becomes method.

In order to undo history's fetishism of the document, to underscore the present as the site in which memory unfolds, and to remind us of the precarity of time and temporality as concepts that belong to both, aurality might offer us a means through which to articulate that which we posit may be thought as the eddying entanglements of Africa and the global mnemoscape. This churning of the global mnemoscape can be read as an effect of an encounter with the discourses of war, colonialism, and genocide when engaged not only from the vantage point of Africa, but through thinking Africa.

It should be said that aurality, or rather a discourse of sound, is not new to studies of the past, but it certainly complicates any universal relation to the past. In fact, it can be argued, and has been, that it is in studies of the past that sound has shown its propensity for excess as well as its inherent critique of a discourse of recovery.[11] Elsewhere, sound and Africa both as place and idea are intertwined in a pursuit of the past. The relationship between aurality and colonialism is at the core of the birth and development of another discipline—ethnomusicology—whose founder Erich Moritz von Hornbostel took it upon himself to record on a phonograph the infamous "Hottentot Venus" Sarah Baartman in order to not only articulate the differences between Western and non-Western physiognomy, but to address what he called the need to "uncover the darkest and most distant past [and] to peel off the timeless and elemental from the fullness of the present."[12]

---

[11] Sound as it has been deployed in the discipline of history has been characterized by a historicist impulse, resulting in a teleology that merely seeks to augment narrative with new aural actors. What is important to note here is the idea that sound is not merely hearing, and that soundscape—a sonic deployment of technologies of mapping—is a critical concept. Daniel Bender, Duane J. Corpis and Daniel J. Walkowitz, "Editor's Introduction: Sound Politics: Critically Listening to the Past," *Radical History Review* 121 (2015): 1–7 (here 3).

[12] The precursor to what becomes ethnomusicology is comparative musicology, and is a discipline not only concerned with music, but how music might grant us insight into the temporal dimensions of culture proper. Eric Ames, "The Sound of Evolution," *Modernism/Modernity* 10 no. 2 (2003): 297–325 (here 298).

Hearing is ironically in many ways the mode through which the law attempts to address and, in rare exceptions, redress offenses against it, which in our discussion here is violence as we call terror and apartheid. In response to these genres of violence Ethiopia and South Africa staged different iterations of "the hearing" in which the former held what is referred to as the Red Terror Trials and the latter held the famous Truth and Reconciliation Commission. Both the Ethiopian Red Terror Trials and the Truth and Reconciliation Commission of South Africa were imagined as "the mode" through which political transition occurs "peacefully," requiring listening and hearing from and to both victims and perpetrators.[13] It is in this sense that these iterations of the legal hearing required a willingness to be activated—to allow the past into the present without fixing it there, so as to listen and to respond to what is being heard with justice in mind. Said differently, to listen here is to endow the law with the quality of activism. It is in this sense that the listening that the legal hearing enables is a potential for a coming to terms with mnemonic legacies of violence.

Hearing, however, also implies mishearing, which is why it must be paired with listening. The term solidarity has at its core an implicit kernel that hints at listening in its etymological trace of communion, and what is required if we are to achieve a mnemoscape entangled in solidarity is a thinking through and from Africa that would produce a democratization of memory discourses. Africa has been lodged as one of the spatial and conceptual others of the West through the discourses of the modern episteme and its effects, not the least of which can be located in area studies and anthropology. Consider, for example, the contemporary trajectory of migrancy that posits the West (and those locales who are marked as its

---

[13] In law trials are usually distinguished from hearings, in the sense that the former is usually a drawn-out procedure in which a definitive and final decision is made after arguments are presented by both parties while the latter is faster in part because its object is to determine a temporary resolution to a matter. However, in the Ethiopian case, the decisions assumed final at Red Terror trials proved temporary in the sense that death penalties were converted to life sentences. Finally, in 2011, 23 members of the Derg serving these life sentences received official pardons by the state. See Yonas Abiye, "Ethiopia Pardons 23 Top Derg Officials," *Ezega News*, June 1, 2011, https://www.ezega.com/News/NewsDetails?NewsID=2919. Debate around the matter of amnesty and pardon had, however, been ongoing since the inception of the retributive mechanism of transitional justice in Ethiopia's inception, see Kjetil Tronvoll, C. Schaefer and Girmachew Alemu Aneme, eds., *The Ethiopian red terror trials: Transitional justice challenged* (New York: Boydell & Brewer, 2009); Girmachew Alemu Aneme, 'Apology and Trials: The Case of the Red Terror Trials in Ethiopia,' *African Human Rights Law Journal* 6 (2006): 64–84.

proxies) as always a destination: that to which is aspired spatially but also (as a consequence of the teachings of modernity) conceptually. The Rest (most of Africa, Asia, South America, etc.) are marked conversely as points of departure: that from which, according to the same epistemic logic, that same trajectory is to spatially and conceptually progress. This is how, through the schizogenic use of time, the discourse of anthropology denies the coevalness of ethnographic fieldwork and produces its object.[14] It is in this sense and through the schizogenic use of time as method that various expressions of the mnemonic discourses of genocide, colonialism, and war have produced their object as knots of memory—both temporally bound and fixed. Said differently, the knot here acts as an anchor, holding in place what remains "there and then"—backwards, primitive, uncivilized—and separating it from the "here and now"—Western, modern/eurocentric, progressive. In "knotting" the Rest and Other of the West with catastrophe, the mnemonic discourses of genocide, war, and colonialism collapse time and space, to produce non-Western nations as perpetually "cold" societies, to borrow from Claude Lévi-Strauss, from whom Jan Assmann develops his theory of "cold" and "hot" memory. In *Cultural Memory and Early Civilization: Writing, Remembrance, and Political Imagination*, Assmann writes that "cold" and "hot" are two poles on the spectrum from primitive to civilized respectively, explaining also that "cold societies do not live by forgetting what hot societies remember—they simply live with a different kind of memory, and in order to do that, they must block out history." From this he posits that cold memories are the nodes of history that mark time, freeze it in place in order for it to be measured. Conversely, hot memory "not only measures out the past, as an instrument of chronological orientation and control, but it also uses past references to create a self-image and to provide support for hopes and for intentions."[15] Hot memory, and indeed hot societies, in this sense use their cold counterparts for creating a self-image—or myth—of superiority and progression, of having developed from where their cold counterparts remain frozen. The deconstruction of this perception of Africa, an example of the democratization to which we referred earlier, requires an understanding of Africa as

---

[14] See Johannes Fabian, *Time and the Other. How Anthropology Makes its Object* (New York: Columbia University Press, 1983).

[15] Jan Assmann, *Cultural Memory and Early Civilization: Writing, Remembrance, and Political Imagination* (Cambridge: Cambridge University Press, 2011), 52, 62; cf Claude Lévi-Strauss, *The Savage Mind* (Chicago: University of Chicago Press, 1966).

a concept and indeed articulating modes of thinking about the world that are non-Eurocentric. What the example of Ethiopia makes clear, furthermore, is that this requires grappling with Africa's unsettling of globally accepted definitions of genocide and colonialism—and in markedly different ways than elsewhere in the world.

Sound, more recently, has become a subject of the south, and is being called upon to do the work of solidarity. Unsurprisingly, it has followed the discursive contours laid out above, as a recent edited collection titled *Remapping Sound Studies* argues in its pursuit of a "Southern Sound Studies." When "south" is defined in the volume, it is not so much a description as it is a genealogy of the term as a rather stable category, with subtle unreferenced nods to both a Marxist revisionist historiography in South Africa (colonialism of a "special type") as well as terms such as "structural adjustment," and institutions such as the World Bank and the International Monetary Fund named. Where it begins with an account of the Enlightenment and Jean-Jacques Rousseau's conflation of sound and south, and the multiple associations with writing, speech, and communication that the *audiovisual litany* marked as ideological, the volume unfortunately returns to the territorialization it began with: the North's other.[16] Once again, Africa is reduced to a site that history happens to—a context.

We are also reminded in rather plain terms, through the idea that the sonic event that is acousmatic is one that betrays its source, that the certainty of the relationship between the source of a sound, its cause, and its effect as sonic emission is not one that translates directly into the listener's experience.[17] In other words, we cannot merely hear if we are to hear properly. We must, and with a political and philosophical urgency, *listen*. Listening is about posture/-*ing* and perspective, a gesture that posits that it is about the movement of the articulated into the visual. It is about a gaze that is not the gaze. We constitute listening here as precisely this work: as activism, as engagement, attentiveness, and action in the moment of turning when we hear the call for a democratization of the global

---

[16] The audiovisual litany is a term coined by Jonathan Sterne and refers to the various differences and dichotomies that surround the senses of sight and hearing. See Jonathan Sterne, *The Audible Past: Cultural Origins of Sound Reproduction* (Durham NC: Duke University Press, 2003), 15. Gavin Steingo and Jim Sykes. "Introduction: Remapping Sound Studies in the Global South," in *Remapping Sound Studies* (Durham NC: Duke University Press, 2019), 1–36.

[17] Brian Kane, *Sound Unseen: Acousmatic Sound in Theory and Practice* (Oxford: Oxford University Press, 2014), 7.

mnemoscape. It is in the act of hearing and listening for and to Africa in a non-reductive sense that we may be able to engage Africa as a productive site from which to think, a site of activation and activism. It is therefore in this sense that we approach Ethiopia and South Africa not as sites of memory, but as mnemonic structures in and of themselves. They do not constitute an alternative to a global mnemoscape nor do they set the stage for a memory studies that would locate itself in Africa or in the global south. Rather, through their disobedience to historicism and to a memory studies that would favor shared remembering as a universal mode of mnemonic discourse, they constitute sites of countercurrents and counterflows.

South Africa: Total War and the Time of War

How might we remember a time of war that is not wartime? How might we listen to the sounds of war misrecognized? The idea of the state of emergency and what is called total war as it unfolds in the context of a settler colonialism that would script the world demands that we consider the formulation colonialism as violence alongside the notion that imperialism is war.[18] What is called the military industrial complex of the South African apartheid state produced the notion of "total war" in relation to the political atmosphere of the Cold War, and this reveals an insecurity around the colonial state, imperial war, and the work of memory. Let us pause for a moment and consider the context of two particular terms that animated both the legal and administrative forces that characterized the various states of emergency in the 1980s in South Africa: total war and militarization. It is through the consideration of these terms as they oscillate in both the historiography and popular memory that we begin to see how temporality itself becomes a marker of insecurity. War, colonialism, and apartheid cease to be discrete objects, periods, or events if we attend to the ways in which these terms move.

By 1976, various events including the Soweto Uprising and the death of anti-apartheid activist Steve Biko in detention in 1977 in particular shifted the political landscape in South Africa and its two key actors, the state and resistance movements, leading to a United Nations arms embargo on South Africa. The discourses of the Cold War and the longstanding

---

[18] See, for example, the idea of global apartheid. See also Jacques Derrida and Peggy Kamuf, "Racism's Last Word," *Critical Inquiry* 12, no. 1 (October 1985): 290–99.

conflation between communism and African nationalism (the red danger and the black danger) in the mind of the apartheid state drove a new administration under P.W. Botha to declare a new state policy in 1979: "total onslaught, total strategy."[19] In July of 1979, Botha would make the infamous "adapt or die" speech, in which he argued for significant reform of the apartheid system if the state in its current form were to survive the current domestic and international situation. Throughout this period, there was a debate both inside and outside the halls of power around whether South Africa *was* indeed at war. At times, the state would argue that it was facing a revolutionary onslaught that required the strategic intervention of the defense forces, and at other times it would state very plainly that the current situation of conflict in the country "involved so many different fronts, unknown to the South African experience, that it has gained the telling but horrifying name of total war." This was captured perhaps in the most telling manner through two specific instances in 1988. The first, which occurred during a treason trial, was a moment where the South African Police noted that the African National Congress could not be thought to be at war with the South African Government and that rather it should be seen in terms of the state facing a "revolutionary onslaught." This argument, according to Jacklyn Cock, was put forward simply to prevent ANC members claiming a prisoner of war status, a status which under the Geneva Protocols of 1977 is granted to those engaged in wars with colonial powers. The second is an instance where in order to circumvent the institution of an order brought by the End Conscription Campaign to restrain the South African Defense Force from harassment, the state argued that because the South African Defense Force (SADF) was on a "war footing," such an intervention was outside of the jurisdiction of the Supreme Court.[20]

---

[19] The idea of the red danger, or *die rooi gevaar*, came to refer to the threat of communism in the language of the apartheid state and its tactical positioning in relation to liberation movements. It also became synonymous with the idea of the black danger, or *die swart gevaar*, a racialized fear of black settlement in white urban areas dating back to the 1930s before the adoption of apartheid policy in 1948. James Selfe "The Total Onslaught and the Total Strategy: Adaptations to the Security Intelligence Decision-Making Structures under P W Botha's Administration" (Unpublished MA thesis, University of Cape Town, 1987), 1–4. For more on the state security apparatus, see James Selfe, "South Africa's National Management System," in *War and Society: The Militarisation of South Africa*, eds. Jaclyn Cock and Laurie Nathan (New York: St. Martin's Press, 1989), 149–58.

[20] Jacklyn Cock, "Introduction," in *War and Society: The Militarisation of South Africa*, eds. Jaclyn Cock and Laurie Nathan (New York: St. Martin's Press, 1989), 1–13 (here 1).

What this series of events did was place the military apparatus in South Africa in a precarious position both inside and outside of politics. Here, militarization was an ideological formation, with its power and influence operating as a social institution with its own networks of cultural memory. What it meant to be at war and to be prepared for war would come to define what the soldier was and what the civilian was, including their own histories of becoming as national identities. It would also, ironically, suture the enemy into the very fabric of that becoming. It was imperialism. It was total war.

It was in this guise of total war that apartheid as a bureaucratic structure would stage its last stand as a series of states of emergency, formalized periods of militarization, and the suspension of human rights in favor of humanitarian principles. More important, however, is that the idea of total war as it unfolds in South Africa (and considering the various military operations of the apartheid state further afield in Southern Africa) reveals to us a temporality around state violence and a relationship to imperialism that must be considered if we are to embark upon the work of entangling memory to achieve a more democratic mnemoscape. To understand how we can constitute a global mnemoscape, we must first look at how the skirmishes of encounter—the small wars of empire that came to constitute the pre-history of South Africa's "total war"—are remembered.

The central feature of the discourse of total war is the inability to name war as anything but one homogenous and discrete temporality, a temporality that cannot but reproduce a teleology that ends in the nation-state, and one that produces a soldier with excess. The Battle of Salt River that would be deemed the inaugural military altercation in South Africa in 1510, is one example which, when attended to, shows up the tension at the heart of this formation. That tension appears not in the historical periodization or narrative structures that govern its retelling in the historiography, but rather in its mnemonic movement: its deployment into cultural memory as a silent marker of what it means to be a soldier in South Africa, and what it means to be a South African soldier. The mnemonic structure that emerges here is a set of ideas and practices surrounding what is called *veldcraft*. As the story goes, Portuguese Viceroy of India Dom Franscisco de Almeida and his men engage an altercation with the indigenous Khoi people of the Cape that results in the death of de Almeida and his crew on the banks of the Salt River (near present-day Cape Town, South Africa) in 1510. The skirmish, which is characterized by a specific "tactic" used by the Khoi—a "phalanx of oxen controlled by whistles and shouts"—is recruited to produce a long historical view of the soldier who must defend the nation, or the warring subject who must protect the nation to come. The altercation, which dissuaded the Portuguese from pursuing any further contact in Southern Africa for another 80 years, would come to mark the onset of a long history of practice of war that cut across the political positioning of competing military forces in the history of conquest and colonialism and resulted in a military practice that draws its key aspects from both colonized and colonizer. This military practice is called *veldcraft*, and according to military historians it is a tactic that underwrites the Dutch *Staatse Leger* (State Army) doctrine, the commando system of the Boers during the South African War in the early 1900s, the regimental system of the Zulu army in the nineteenth century, Basotho horsemen and the modern South African soldier of the 1980s—all subsumed into a single narrative of a national and geopolitically specific military strategy.[21] The South African soldier is born out of *veldcraft*, and *veldcraft* is the inaugural mnemonic discourse that becomes practice in the service of total war.

What we might call the mnemonic fragment that is the Khoi leading their livestock in military formation with non-vocal vocalizations is transformed into tactic: its recollection, remembering, and calling into service directly subsumed into a discourse of practice, and critically, a practice, technique, and indeed apparatus that operates within the logic of defense and is by definition *warring*. It now cannot be rendered as anything other than this, and its recollection is bound to the state and to a particular temporality associated with war. It is a practice however, that not only produces a long history of warring in Southern Africa but also produces a mnemonic discourse around land, voice, war, and the indigenous. It is in the land that cannot speak and must be spoken for (read, read) that the Khoi are subsequently buried *through* the transformation of this memory into practice.[22] It is through what is called *veldcraft*—the very name

---

[21] Willem P. Steenkamp, "The Shaping of the South African Soldier, 1510–2008," *Journal for Contemporary History* 34, no. 1 (2009): 207–22.

[22] It is also ironic that the Battle of Salt River is also called the first war of resistance against European aggressors, with former state president Thabo Mbeki invoking it in relation to his project of African Renaissance which argued for an intellectual renewal of Africa. It is also in this sense that the category of *veldcraft* should be thought alongside ethnographic histories of indigeneity in South Africa, where the relationship between the Khoi and the San (often referred to by the derogatory term 'Bushman') to land and nature is one marked by a conflation which is at the heart of the exclamation that the San are historically the closest to

replaces the Anglicized *bush* with its more located Afrikaans term, *veld*, implying control and dominion—that the memory of the Khoi and their aurality would travel in time and through time, timelessly.[23] When this mnemonic fragment becomes a tactic, it transforms into a vehicle—a technique—for remembering that is practiced in relation to power. We might observe the ways in which historiography facilitates this process as the production of tradition; the Khoi disappear into their aural markers (the whistles and shouts) and indigenous tradition remains but only as warring. The small war of 1510 is subsumed into total war, unwittingly revealing to us the discursive traces that make up an untenable concept of war and a wartime that only history can hold.

The soldier must be the recipient of a nascent wartime, not only to carry the temporalities of the past into uncertain futures but also to embody its rhythm that is both *kairos* and *chronos*, both in time and on time. It comes to mark his or her body in the wake of unspeakable violence. It comes as no surprise that the transition—which was in itself a movement from a state of emergency to an emergent state—was haunted by how South Africa might resolve a crisis of military institution. What was a postapartheid army to look like and act, given the horrific reputation the South African army had crafted for itself both in Africa and abroad? How would it resolve the various categories of defender of the nation, categories that included insurgent, commandant, terrorist, and conscript?[24]

The latter is not a question that will be addressed here, but it points to another matter, that is, the ways in which the tension at the heart of the inability to name war in South Africa may have a longer if not more encompassing genesis. Adam Sitze reminds us that imperial war—often described as the "small wars" of empire and taking place in what is regarded in the metropole as peacetime—is critical to the very theoretical base of

---

humanity's earliest ancestors. See David Johnson, *Imagining the Cape Colony: History, Literature, and the South African Nation* (Cape Town: University of Cape Town Press, 2012), 10–34.

[23] On the ways in which the idea of tribe and native congeal in the production of the Afrikaner and its stakes for considering identity politics, race, and nationalism in South Africa, see Suren Pillay, "Where do you belong? Natives, foreigners and apartheid South Africa," *African Identities* 2, no. 2 (2004): 215–32.

[24] See Lephophotho Mashike, "'Blacks Can Win Everything, but the Army': The 'Transformation' of the South African Military between 1994 and 2004," *Journal of Southern African Studies* 33, no. 3 (2007): 601–18.

empire as such.²⁵ Mary Dudziak emphasizes the relation between wartime and peacetime, and how this has effects not only in the realm of law, but also on the discipline of history by considering the ways in which the onset of war marks not an event but an era that is temporary.²⁶ What Dudziak alerts us to is the ways in which war is textured by an eventness that exceeds event. It is no surprise therefore that war is a barometric structure for empire itself, as Sitze tells us; it not only provides the terms upon which to determine the overall health and status of an imperial endeavor, but also affects how empire thinks about justice, morality, and its ultimate goal. It is that which gives imperialism its meaning, its ultimate philosophical force. Interestingly, considering the ways in which apartheid has been theorized as an economic system designed to exploit the labor of black bodies and furthermore as an articulation of a neoliberal ideal, Sitze argues that there is a fundamental contradiction at the heart of imperial war that the imperial administrator must manage: a dialectic between war and capital. In essence, imperial war must save imperialism from its own suicidal drive.²⁷ It serves to defer its own death. What can a time of war that is not wartime tell us about imperial time? How is the work of remembering—that is, suturing the relationship between the past and present—to take place in the wake of such a complicated relationship between the historicity of the present and a historicism of the past?

It was, after all, the fall of the Berlin Wall that not only ushered in the end of apartheid as a legal system but also a concept of historicity that would seek to reify the past as unchanging, unshifting, and static. It would also be the period that would give birth to memory studies proper. This historicity, which bears the battle scars of a modernist paradigm, cannot think the way memory does: in the present and with a drive toward reconstitution. The rise of a temporality—a mnemonic structure in and of itself—interested in how the past (re)-presents the present is one that uncovers for us the ways in which war and its scripts become visible. What we are calling the military industrial complex of the apartheid state—that network of state, violence, and world-historical force—is in fact total war: imperialism proper.

---

²⁵ Adam Sitze, "The Imperial Critique of Imperial War," *Filosofia Politica* 25, no. 2 (August 2011): 315–34 (here 316).
²⁶ Mary L. Dudziak, *War-Time: An Idea, Its History, Its Consequences* (New York: Oxford University Press, 2012).
²⁷ Sitze, "The Imperial Critique," 333.

This is an argument we can only make now, in this present, given the ways in which the memory of wartime in South Africa is unresolved and contested. It is through wartime that the nation can be and is imagined in the present; an imagining that collapses the various divisions between colonial conquest, states of emergency, and global war. We can explore this most prominently in the example of the sunken troopship the *SS Mendi*, whose memory has been invoked multiple times in contemporary South African politics to imagine a long unbroken history of the quintessential South African soldier.[28] In particular, the *SS Mendi* becomes metonymic for the black soldier, or the infantrymen of the South African Native Labour Contingent: a battalion of black soldiers sent as labor to the frontlines in World War I, to not only face a war unarmed but to be the subjects of a testing ground for segregation.[29] The iconic moment of the death drill—when a certain Reverend Isaac Dyobha led soldiers on the sinking ship in a dance of death—is central to the retelling of the narrative of the sinking of the *SS Mendi*. The death drill, as it is often recalled, is one that calls forth a unified, multiracial and multicultural national subject, and interweaves it into the figure of the soldier who must defend the nation to come. Dyobha led the men with the following invocation:

> Be quiet and calm, my countrymen, for what is taking place is exactly what you came to do. You are going to die … but that is what you came to do… Brothers, we are drilling the death drill. I, a Xhosa, say you are my brothers. Swazis, Pondos, Basutos, we die like brothers. We are the sons of Africa. Raise your war cries, brothers, for though they made us leave our assegais in the kraal, our voices are left with our bodies.

In an act of re-membering, the death drill has found itself at the center of a novel titled *Dancing the Death Drill* by author Fred Khumalo dramatizing a black recruit of mixed racial heritage surviving the tragic sinking. The narrative hinges on its opening salvo: an unprecedented violent act in a Parisian restaurant is figured as an outburst of latent anger harbored from a betrayal as the *SS Mendi* sank. The betrayal is explored through a

---

[28] John Gribble and Graham Scott, *We Die Like Brothers: The Sinking of the SS Mendi* (Swindon: Historic England, 2017); Albert Grundlingh, "Mutating Memories and the Making of a Myth: Remembering the SS Mendi Disaster, 1917–2007," *South African Historical Journal* 63, no. 1 (2011): 20–37 (here 31).

[29] See Brian P. Willan, "The South African Native Labour Contingent, 1916–1918," *The Journal of African History* 19, no. 1 (1978): 61–78.

reimagining of the complicity of the captain of the *Darro*, who refused to help the *SS Mendi* because of its black crew. In an almost foreboding sense, the tragedy is inserted into a network of collective memory closely tied to the idea of South Africanness born out of the transformation from traumatic memory into narrative memory that was the discursivity of the Truth and Reconciliation Commission.[30] The *SS Mendi* and the moment that comes to be associated with it—the dancing of the death drill as the ship sank—is immortalized in Khumalo's novel Fred Khumalo not only through its title, but in the ways in which the death drill becomes the core temporal narrative device through which the novel simultaneously attempts to work through the tragic circumstances of the sinking of the *SS Mendi* and make sense of its return as a temporal object in the postapartheid present. In the final scene of the novel, the protagonist deploys the death drill—that sonically charged mnemonic device—as the quintessential structure of subject formation:

> "I am dancing my death drill. No one can take it away from me. This death drill is my truth. They made me leave my spear, my shield, back home those many years ago. So I am going to fight with my words, turn my words into bullets. This dance is my history, my heritage, my story that they tried to suppress. This is my death drill, my dance of death, my dance of truth." Like the men on the Mendi, he danced, the rhythmic slamming of feet gaining momentum with each movement. Slam-slam! Slam-slam![31]

A specific articulation of wartime has provided the script through which the warring subject forces the past into the present, in ways that uncannily replicate the scripts of a historicity that would seek a teleological resolution. This resolution is made on the warring subject. What we are construing as war is memory masquerading as history, a linear, homogenous and causal notion of time that cannot move freely.

Conclusion

What is being termed solidarity is a manner through which to account for a flattening of the mnemonic landscape—intended or otherwise. This flattening has at its core a desire to constitute a world that remembers

---

[30] Cf Paul Gilroy, "Lecture I. Suffering and infrahumanity lecture II. Humanities and a new humanism," *Tanner Lectures* (2014): 69.

[31] Fred Khumalo, *Dancing the Death Drill* (Cape Town: Umuzi, 2017), 335.

collectively, that puts its past together in moves that must be named solidarity. To entangle memory therefore is to constitute a temporality that might transcend the notion of progress that world history has given us as the ideal script. What the examples of Ethiopia and South Africa reveal is that attention must be directed toward the notion of the apparatus: juridical, imperial, mnemonic, disciplinary, technological, or otherwise. Thinking in terms of apparatus could be constitutive not only of how we might approach mnemonic solidarity as a call, but also how it is we might reckon with Africa in the moment of such a hailing. Indeed, what was made apparent in our examples was the question of technique: a working on the subject that cannot be neatly subsumed into what has been called the global mnemoscape. For example, Ethiopia proves critical if we are to think the mnemonic through its technicality; the Ethiopian Red Terror as an example of genocide sits precisely within that work of memory called forgetting. It is that expression of genocide, within a space never colonized, that genocide studies largely refuses to remember. What is at stake in the Ethiopian example of the eddying of genocide and terror—of the swirling, mixing, and churning of two distinct violations of international law—is the question of the lived, human experience of the atrocities that still-now sear of their everyday. The Ethiopian Red Terror is largely *forgotten* within the discourse of genocide; and yet remains *always present* in the memory of those who lived through and survived it. It is in relation to this that the desire for mnemonic solidarity and the democratization of the mnemonic discourses of genocide, colonialism, and war is a desire for abiding by the fluidity of memory. Said differently, it is a desire that gestures toward making the practice those discourses not *knotting* but *eddying*.

Similarly, it is the uncertainty of memory as it is deployed to do the work of history that comes to churn the mnemonic in the case of South Africa. If temporality comes to mark the history of war in South Africa, it is because the soldier is a subject that travels across time and complicates how we configure war and its conceptual and discursive histories on the continent. The soldier is the subject that neither history nor memory can hold alone and is therefore a troubling prospect for a mnemoscape which must exceed the nation in its shape. It is precisely because total war and militarization cannot but must sit alongside each other that we are forced to recognize that perhaps what is considered universal must instead be thought as undemocratic. What mnemonic solidarity might then mean is an attentiveness to movement rather than situatedness. We are compelled to read a global mnemoscape on the grounds of churning rather than entanglement. It is in the techniques through which memory is recruited to make sense of the disjointed time of war that we notice the intertwining of the work of history and memory. The whistle and shout and the death drill are both sonic mnemonic apparatuses that are both memory and transformed into memory and set to work to make sense of how the soldier and its excessive subjectivity can be held in a larger national narrative.

The noun memory is, as we know, intrinsically entangled with the past, but when put to work, indeed sounded out a verb, it defies its temporal limits and when recalled it is once again present. Memory in the singular is a condensation of fragmented remnants of lives, histories, and narratives—individual and collective, trans-generationally and locally textured. It is this capacity of the human that has germinated a field of study, and it is beyond the scope of this chapter to debate what precisely the work of memory studies is. Rather this chapter is concerned with how it is that the discourses of genocide, war, and colonialism contour the mnemoscape in ways that resist the neatness of rendering the objects of any of these discourses discrete. It is a gesture toward working through the desire for the deterritorialization of the mnemoscape, as simultaneously contextually sanded by the local and global, but not universal. To put it another way, this chapter looks toward a democratization of the global mnemoscape that is not inherently liberal. To do so we turn to Africa as not a cartographic and geological location but as a concept and methodology.

Open Access This chapter is licensed under the terms of the Creative Commons Attribution 4.0 International License (http://creativecommons.org/licenses/by/4.0/), which permits use, sharing, adaptation, distribution and reproduction in any medium or format, as long as you give appropriate credit to the original author(s) and the source, provide a link to the Creative Commons licence and indicate if changes were made.

The images or other third party material in this chapter are included in the chapter's Creative Commons licence, unless indicated otherwise in a credit line to the material. If material is not included in the chapter's Creative Commons licence and your intended use is not permitted by statutory regulation or exceeds the permitted use, you will need to obtain permission directly from the copyright holder.

Index[1]

A
Afro-pessimism, 51
Anne Frank (as icon), 1, 25, 26, 31, 32
Anti-fascism, 92
Antisemitism, 20–24, 29, 33, 46, 55–65, 58n27, 67, 69, 70
Apology, politics of, 95
Aurality/sound studies, 10, 115, 116, 124
Australia, 93

B
Baltic states, 95
  Lithuania, 20, 21
Bandung, 3
Bataan, 31
Bataclan Night Club bombing 2015, 11
Black Lives Matter, 51
Brexit, 51

C
Canada, 24, 50, 93
Catholicism, 32
China, 3, 8, 12n19, 31, 74, 75, 90, 92, 93, 96, 101, 102
Cities and local memory, 5, 10–12, 38
Cold War, 4, 16–19, 30, 42, 65, 92, 93, 120
Colonialism, 7, 16–43, 46, 47, 53, 54, 61, 66, 69, 71, 106–109, 115, 116, 118, 119, 120, 123, 128, 129
  and Holocaust/Nazism, 16–43, 54, 66, 71
Comfort women, 3, 4, 11, 16, 31, 34–40, 73–104
Compensation/reparations, 36, 79, 80, 87, 88, 94, 95, 99–101, 103
Concentration camps, 5, 20, 49–52, 57, 57n25, 59, 78n4, 82
  Auschwitz, 78
  Dachau, 50
  Jasenovac, 5

[1] Note: Page numbers followed by 'n' refer to notes.

Crimea, 91
Crimes against humanity, 38, 62, 76–78, 83n16, 99–100, 110, 113–115
  Rome Statute of the International Criminal Court (1998), 78, 110
Czechoslovakia/Czechia, 21, 67

D
Diasporas
  African; African Americans, 3, 24, 25, 49, 50, 51n11, 52, 53, 58, 87; Afropeans, 48, 53, 54
  Armenian Americans, 35, 36
  Japanese Americans, 3, 36, 82n14
  Korean Americans, 35, 37, 93

E
East Timor, 83
Ethiopia
  Derg regime, 110
  Red Terror, 105, 107–109, 111–113, 117, 117n13, 128

F
Filipino, 30
Films, 25, 31, 45, 48, 52, 52n14, 53, 63, 79, 82n15
France (Vichy), 64, 78, 92, 98

G
Genocide
  Armenian genocide, 34, 35, 37, 40, 40n73
  Convention on the Crime of Genocide 1948, 114
  Rwandan genocide, 37, 81

German Federal Republic, 4, 7, 18, 19, 21–26, 30, 38, 41, 42, 48–51, 52n14, 54, 56–59, 61, 63, 63n43, 66, 76, 78, 91, 95, 98, 109, 115, 115n10
Global South, 3, 4, 7–9, 13, 16, 70, 120
Greece, 29
Gwangju Uprising 1980, 11

H
Habsburg Empire, 66, 67
Hibakusha (A-bomb survivors), 27, 29, 31, 33
Hillsborough Stadium Disaster 1996, 13
Hiroshima, 1, 3, 4, 27, 29–31, 92
Historikerstreit, 18, 41, 42
Holocaust, 1, 4–8, 5n2, 16–43, 46, 55–67, 69–71, 77–79, 81, 82n13, 85, 87, 94n37, 95, 97, 100, 103, 115
  Black victims, 4, 48–54, 69
Human rights, 4, 8, 9, 12n18, 27, 37, 39, 46–48, 65n47, 70, 71, 78, 79, 83, 88, 89, 94–96, 99–101, 103, 110, 122
Hungary, 29, 67, 68, 74

I
Iceland, 27
Imperialism, 18, 30, 66, 71, 98, 120, 122, 125
India, 24, 65, 66, 69, 74, 122
Indonesia (incl. Batavia), 30
Israel/Palestine
  anti-Zionism, 58
  Boycott, Disinvestment, Sanctions movement, 58

INDEX

J
Japan, 3, 8, 27, 29, 30, 32, 33, 35, 38, 39, 74–76, 79, 80, 84n19, 84n20, 88, 91–97, 99–103
Jews, 8n12, 19, 21, 24–27, 40n73, 42, 55–60, 59n32, 62–64, 66, 78, 81, 95
Justice/law (s.a.) tribunals
 commemorative, 2, 80
 compensatory, 2, 80
 performative, 76, 80
 restorative, 2, 78, 80

K
Katyn Massacre 1940, 30
Korea, 8, 31, 34, 35, 37–39, 74, 75, 80, 83, 88, 89, 92–98, 94n38, 101–103, 102n55

L
Labour Party (UK), 56, 60, 63
Latin America
 Argentina, 7
 Chile, 7
 Mexico, 36, 57
 Peru, 27

M
Melancholia, 8, 46–72
Memory
 cold and hot, 118
 cosmopolitan memory, 5, 6, 17, 29–31, 35, 36, 39–41
 global memory culture, 76, 97, 100–104
 global memory formation, 2–4, 6, 8, 10, 11, 16, 18, 40–42
 morphemes of memory, 50
 multidirectional memory, 5, 40, 46, 48, 55, 62
 place memory, 12
 prosthetic memory, 5
 rights of memory, 87–89
 screen memory, 5, 17, 18, 18n5, 22, 31, 40
 transcultural memory, 5
 transnational memory, 6, 11, 91, 95, 101, 103
 traveling memory, 5
Migration/migrants, 34, 46, 47, 52, 53, 57, 57n25, 60, 66, 70
 See also Refugees
Mnemonic solidarity, 1–13, 18, 36–38, 41, 48, 57, 61, 70, 71, 107, 108, 115, 128
Mongolia, 27
Multicultural(ism), 71
Museums, 26, 38, 58, 105
Muslims/Islam, 3, 36, 59, 66, 67
 Islamophobia, 20, 22

N
Nagasaki, 4, 26–33, 40
Nanjing Massacre, 4, 16, 75, 82n13, 90, 91, 93, 97–98
Nationalism
 ethno-nationalism, 56, 59, 65
 hate nationalism, 102
 performative nationalism, 11, 34–39
 victimhood nationalism, 29, 39
National Socialism (Nazism), 42
Native Americans, 3, 16
Neo-liberalism, 70
Netherlands/Dutch, 26, 77, 80, 93, 123
Novels, 24, 32, 33, 48, 50, 51, 55, 63, 79, 126–127

O
Orientalism, 20

P
Pakistan, 65
Philippines, 83, 88n27, 94n38
Philo-Semitism, 61
Poland, 19–24, 22n14, 26, 27, 30, 33, 67, 92, 95
Populism, 54, 60, 70
Postcolonialism, 24, 41
Post-postracial, 51, 51n11

R
Race/whiteness, 20, 25, 28, 30, 49, 52, 54, 55, 58, 71, 124n23
Refugees, 19, 20, 22, 22n14, 66–68
Religion, 20, 28
Responsibility, 8, 42, 61, 76, 80, 83n17, 97–100, 104
Roma ("Gypsies"), 66, 69, 71
Russia, 20, 74, 91, 91n35, 92, 95, 113
Rwanda, 77, 100

S
Sewol Ferry Disaster 2014, 13
Sexual violence/rape, 3, 37, 77, 80, 82, 83, 88, 96, 101, 103
See also Comfort women
Singapore, 29
Slavery, 4, 9, 16, 24, 34, 36–39, 48, 50, 53, 54, 56, 69, 83, 83n17, 84, 87, 94, 95, 98, 99, 101
South Africa, 9, 10, 25, 26, 32, 78, 88, 106, 107, 108, 113, 115, 117, 119, 120–128
  apartheid, 9, 10, 25, 32, 88, 107, 108, 117, 120, 121, 124n23
Soviet Union/Gulag, 40, 91, 92

SS Mendi, 126, 127
Statues and memorials, 93

T
Taiwan, 90, 93
Television broadcasts, 49
Territorialization
  de-territorialization, 4, 6, 40
  re-territorialization, 4, 6, 7, 10, 17, 70
Terror, 4, 7, 10, 13n23, 17, 18, 40, 42, 105, 106, 108–115, 117, 128
Trianon, Treaty of, 67
Tribunals (s.a. justice, Truth and Reconciliation)
  Eichmann Trial, 78
  International Criminal Court for Rwanda, 77
  International Criminal Tribunal for the Former Yugoslavia, 37, 79
  International War Crimes Tribunal on Japan's Military Sexual Slavery 2000, 37
  Nuremberg War Crimes Tribunal, 76
  Red Terror Trials (Ethiopa), 117
  Tokyo War Crimes Tribunal, 76
Truth
  right to, 89, 99
  Truth and Reconciliation Commissions, 78, 117, 127
Turkey, 74

U
Ukraine/*Holodomor*, 16
United Kingdom, 51, 53
United Nations (UN), 25, 65, 89, 89n30, 93, 94, 99, 101, 101n54, 110, 120
Urakami Cathedral, 28

V

Vertreibung (post-1945 expulsions of Germans), 16
Victimhood
  hierarchy/competition, 19, 40, 71
  nationalism, 11, 29, 31, 39, 41
Vietnam, 16, 29

W

Wars
  Pacific War, 30, 92
  in South Africa memory, Battle of Salt River, 122, 123n22
  total war, 92, 97, 98, 120–121, 128
  Vietnam War, 16, 29

World War II, 21, 29, 34, 36, 74, 79–81, 90, 90n34, 91, 95–97, 100
Warsaw Ghetto, 25
Windrush Scandal, 51
Witnessing/speech, 3, 10, 11, 25, 27, 28, 35, 37, 40n73, 56, 64, 81, 91, 96, 99, 102, 111, 112, 119, 121
World Trade Center Bombing 2001, 13

Y

Yad Vashem, 5
Yasukuni Shrine, 75, 91, 102n56
Yugoslavia/Balkans/Bosnia, 3, 5, 29, 37, 77, 79

The manufacturer's authorised representative in the EU is Springer Nature Customer Service Centre GmbH, Europaplatz 3, 69115 Heidelberg, Germany. If you have any concerns regarding our products, please contact ProductSafety@springernature.com

Printed and bound by CPI Group (UK) Ltd, Croydon, CR0 4YY
23/03/2026
02076401-0006